The Chicano Treatise

Julián Segura Camacho

UNIVERSITY PRESS OF AMERICA,® INC.

Lanham • Boulder • New York • Toronto • Oxford

Copyright © 2005 by
University Press of America,® Inc.
4501 Forbes Boulevard
Suite 200
Lanham, Maryland 20706
UPA Acquisitions Department (301) 459-3366

PO Box 317
Oxford
OX2 9RU, UK

Library of Congress Control Number: 2004106990
ISBN 0-7618-2923-7 (paperback : alk. ppr.)
ISBN 978-0-7618-2923-2

Contents

Introduction   v

1   Mestizo: An Apology for Being Indio   1

2   The Greatest Fabrication: La Virgen de Guadalupe   11

3   The Myth of Machismo   19

4   The Pimpification of Mexico's Export Labor Class: Mexican Workers In The US Are Prostituted For Mexico's Elite   27

5   The False Illusion of the Chicano/Mexicano Family   35

6   The Generation Divide: Chicano Movement Armchair Revolutionaries Wage War on New Bucks   49

7   The Betrayal   59

8   The Honest Truth About Sexual Prowlness: Chicanos & Chicanas Are Alike   65

9   An Alternative Home: Non-Mexicans Finding Acceptance Among Mexicans   71

10   Afterthought   79

Notes   81

Introduction

The written words of *The Chicano Treatise* originated from a stagnant thought process rooted in the academic institutions and the very individuals attempting to analyze issues Mexicans confront on a daily basis.

This book views Mexicans from northern Mexico, now called The United States of America by a Mexican born and raised in California. The focus is an inner perspective from someone not privileged nor gifted by educational and economic channels; a by-product of Mexican segregation in the United States of America yet still hobbled by historical poverty from Mexico.

The seed was sowed in the history classes at UCLA where I realized that the majority of the White faculty did not know what they were saying about Mexicans, both historically and contemporaneously. As I became a faculty member at East Los Angeles College in the Chicano Studies department, I realized the Chicano faculty were generally acting as parrots (except for Frank Gutier-rez-many thought he was too "Indioed out"), repeating what they had been force fed by these "expert universities".

The first essay was therefore an analysis of the racial caste construct of the word, "Mestizo", the process is to therefore deconstruct a misapplied term. Second, because the conquest of Efpaña was simultaneously physical and spiritual, Mexican Catholicism has to be understood within the confines of war and showcased as a perpetual usurper of Mexican spirituality. Third, *The Chicano Treatise* is not solely a historical argument, rather a continual examination of current Mexican life in the United States. The myth of machismo expands the simple argument of Mexican men as overbearing individuals. Instead, I demonstrate that gender geography is a more comprehensive approach when discussing men and women. American feminism has successfully villainized Mexican men without acknowledging the power women have and the exact oppression men must confront in this society. Sadly, an individual thought process has not taken root among some of the new Chicano thinkers, allowing outsiders to dictate the vocabulary.

The pimpification of Mexico's export labor class can easily be constructed as an argument of transborder, but as history demonstrates, Mexico has never been separated from the north (USA): geographically, spatially, culturally, economically and demographically. Therefore, the proximity of two artificial countries relegates its most vulnerable citizenry to dangers and yet, compensation is extracted to the local pueblos as a viable corporate structure that benefits the elites in Mexico.

Chapter five is a scope into taboos, family or lack of, and incest. Family differences, abuses, even hatred that exist among Mexicans. This is not about airing laundry, (it is already hanging from the clothesline) but about discussing the positives and negatives that "loved ones" commit to each other.

Chapter six on the generational divide is at the heart of this inspiration. The angle presented here is how older Chicanos who benefited from the minimal era of "affirmative action" have been the first to close doors on the post 1970s generation of Mexicans. This is a critique of the past acting in the present.

Chapter seven titled, "The Betrayal" aims to reunite extra-cash Mexicans who fall prey to the false notions of the American Dream via private education. Their lack of interest in public education can create future schisms for the most in need, children.

The second to last chapter is a sexual discussion rarely displayed out in public. Because of the historical legacy of Christian sin, what ancient Mexicans celebrated as fertility dances and worship with no shame in the human body, are now repressed thoughts. Besides religious notions of sexual sin, in the last fifty-years, Mexicans on both sides of the border have been portrayed as sexual beasts with no control, though White Americans still outnumber Mexicans almost two to one. Every sexual sin is frequently attached to Mexicans: teenage pregnancy, demographic growth, large families and children born out of wedlock. Even the media portrays Mexicans negatively by rarely displaying positive sex scenes, outside the maid being taken advantage of. This is a coming out chapter that counters the stereotypes.

The final chapter is an alternative to the Black-White paradigm. I argue that Mexicans may be the best alternative to the endless foundation of social division. Mexicans are defined by culture versus color. We are categorized not by a color rather by heterogeneous cultures that are multi-lingual, culturally creative, musically inspiring and geographically rooted. After all, we Mexicans have never left our homeland; our ruins, customs, and dead are still present in the soil.

To conclude, a series of recommendations are presented at the end of the book as a sense of human hope and greater comprehension. If we cannot create our own cultural discourses, we as a future are doomed.

Muchas gracias to Alicia Jimenez who edited *The Chicano Treatise*, Marcos Ramos (Mi carnal from Berkeley) and all of those who I pestered, *chingé* for attention and had input from. *Los quiero un chingo!*

Chapter One

Mestizo: An Apology
For Being Indio

TODAY

The arrival and subsequent conquest of Mexicans by Christians
via Spain, and the syncretism of both Mexican and Christian-
Catholic cultures has theoretically resulted in a glorification of the
Mestizo; half Indian-half Spaniard.

As it is understood, Indian is an inappropriate-descriptive term
for the people of *México*, the Caribbean and the whole continent.
For people with brown skin from *México* and the United States
this is a mistaken description. I will use the term Mexican to mean
Native American in an all-encompassing manner for North America. Moreover, I will also use names of other nations to be more
precise. For example, on my father's side of the family are
Maayos from outside *Los Mochis*, *Sinaloa* and from my mother's
side, they are *Purempechas* from outside of *León, Guanajuato*
who all migrated to the land of the *Cucapahs* in the *Cachanilla*
Valley of *Mexicali, Baja California* and Imperial County.

DETACHED

I have always struggled in comprehending my space, place and
time in connection to my ethnicity as both a Chicano with the

status of Caucasian and as an American citizen. From my Mexican past, there was an understanding that we were *Mestizos*. Both bloods were equally present. The modern Mexican had arrived via the Spanish language and Catholicism. As I read about the modern Mexican—a half-breed—I became concerned with the fact that Mexicans are both Native Americans and Spaniard. Yet, Spaniards were not Mexicans. Why did we accept them? Why did they reject us? The Mexican became the peasant and for the last five hundred years. We have traversed not only through stages of peasantry but as wandering *Mexicas* through old and modern *México*; both central and northern into what we now call the United States of America, rural and urban and in-between, the Southwest *Aztlan*.

PHYSICAL HISTORY

I searched. Who was I? I intentionally traveled to all the old cities that may be asleep but not dead. *Uruapan, Pátzcuaro, Teotihuacán, Chichen Itzá, Uxmal, Tulum, Machu Pichuu, Tikal, Cuzco, Sacsahuaman, Pizaq, Ollantaytambo, Tiwanaku, Copacabana, El Lago Titicaca, México D. F., Chuquiago, Chuquisaca, Mexicali, Yangna, Taos, Casa Grande* are pueblos, barrios and more pueblos. There I only confirmed what had always been evident: the *Mexica* was not dead and we were not half-breeds. Though an excursion confirmed my conviction. Spain was Moorish and Roman, but not Mexican. Therefore, I was not Spanish, Roman or Moorish. I was a Maayo and a *Purempecha* from the lands now called *México* and the United States of America.

DEMOGRAPHICS

My visit to Spain validated my assumption—I was Mexican. But, why was the notion of a half-breed, a mestizo the accepted norm? Domination and Catholicism transformed *Mexicas* into peasants:

gente floja, ignorante, sucia e incapaz (lazy, ignorant, dirty and incapable people). Mexicans in pure numbers sense never were *mestizos*. The categorization and the spreading of the *mestizo* myth revolves around the Catholics semi-acceptance of possible converts to build or work the entrepreneurial camps known as missions, or monasteries and then Christ. The church openly encouraged marriage between Spaniards and Mexicans but how many Christians really settled in *México*? The figures indicate there were 120,000 in the first century of Christian rule. There were also just as many Africans enslaved in *México* during that time, another 120,000. In comparison, as the holocaust engulfed this land and the cattle killed the fertile fields, Mexicans still accounted for a population of somewhere between 1 and 4 million people. This without doubt was an undercount as many historians have pinpointed. I believe 6 million to be more of an appropriate estimate. How did we continue to survive and maintain native languages? The U.S. census of today, year 2000 even with technology has major shortcomings in the accurate tabulation of Mexicans whether U.S. citizen or not.

The racial and social classes indicate the order of colonial *México*.

1. *Peninsulares*
2. *Criollos*
3a. *Mestizos*
3b. *Indios*
3c. *Negros* (Blacks)

Those individuals who were born in Spain comprise category 1. Individuals who were born in *México* and were also children of individuals who were born in Spain comprise Category 2. Mestizos, Indians and Blacks were considered to be at the bottom of the hierarchy, categories 3, 4, and 5. Here is the question: Why would the conqueror marry the conquered one?

First of all, most had wives back in Spain and eventually brought them to live in *México*. Racial discrimination was instantaneous.

The *Peninsulares* thought themselves superior. They did rape. Such abuse of power occurs in all wars, conquests, etc.

Second, the difference was also based on class. A racial and class difference would serve to discourage any conjugation other than through rape? The offspring of such rape or semi-open relationship would result in children. The mestizos! Who did some of these children stay with? They stayed with the father, a Spanish father that probably had a wife back in Spain. How could a few men repopulate the whole *Cem Anahuac*—the one world? Those children that remained with the Mexican mother never spoke *Castellano*, because the mother spoke *Nahuatl* or *Purempecha*. Even the Spaniards utilized Mexican—*Nahuatl* to attempt to unify all the Mexicans from the new controlled territories.

Mestizos and Mexicans were the same people. There were no half-breeds, as we know it. This is similar to segregation. Even in contemporary Los Angeles, very few Anglos intermarry with Mexicans. In essence, *mestizaje* would mean that the whole population would have to have been fifty-fifty and maintain itself fifty-fifty through the centuries. This was not the case. There was more *mestizaje* with Africans, perhaps because there were more African men than African women available. The African men reproduced with Mexican women but after one generation, only a limited number of African men were brought into *México* due to the high expense of the slave trade. The children as adults themselves reproduced with other non-mixed Mexicans. Limited strains remained. There were more Spaniards that migrated to *México* from 1936-1939 because of the Spanish civil war than they did during the first one hundred years of Christian rule. Even then, those Spaniards, which migrated in the 20th century, have remained insular.

The Spaniards brought their overseers, some judges and those who could not be kings in Spain. There was a plantation, hacienda and *estancia* structure, depending on geography. Most Mexicans were not taught to speak or write Spanish as can be seen from the literacy campaigns in the 20th century. I do distinguish though between Spanish speaking Mexicans and *Nahuatl* speaking Mexicans. The Spanish speaking were few enough to communicate with the masses. Most priests also learned *Nahuatl* because it was easier to communicate rather than instruct *Caxteyano— Castellano* to Mexicans.

The brutally imposed Christianity conversion of Mexicans did not demonstrate *mestizaje* as we know it. Becoming Christian was generally a matter of survival. Yes, I accept *Cristo* and the *Virgen María*. These were foreign symbols to Mexicans, thus to accept Christ was a matter of remaining alive. The friars were continuously frustrated at the endless discovery of *Mexica* symbols and deities in Catholics shrines or temples. They tried continuously and endlessly to convert them. Initially they baptized them. As Mexicans were baptized, the *padrino* (godfather), either the priest or even the new lord of the land would pick the child's first name. One became *José, Jesús, Gerardo, Gonzalo*, and *Tomás*.

The friars in addition utilized the saints' names given in the Christian calendar, which resembled the *panteón* of *Mexica* spiritual leaders or gods. This practice of being named after the patron (saint) day of birth was the norm for Mexicans. One's names would have been *13 Cimi* (day 13 of death) and so forth. The Mexicans understood the new calendar to represent such practice. It is no coincidence that the most common Mexican names in the 20th century continue to be, *José, María, Guadalupe, Jesús, Miguel, Teresa, Lourdes, Pedro, Francisco* and *Antonio*. Slave names! These are all Spanish Christian names. Had the conquerors been the Moors we would instead be using, Ibrahim, Mohamed, Abdul, Tarik and so forth. This is seen in Indonesia, the Philippines and most recently among Mexicans in Los Angeles who have converted to Islam. Professor John Morales of Los Angeles Mission College states in his Chicano Studies History courses of early Mexican Spanish Colonialism that most Spanish names now currently accepted as the norm among Mexicans and Chicanos are slave names by way of forced conversion. The alternative was the Holy Office of the Inquisition, to be burned at the stake. Christianity, Christian names and Jesus symbols never existed in *México* until 1521.

Therefore, just because one accepted a foreign religion and a semi new tongue, *Castellano* does not mean that one has come from that place of origin. I would further argue that Mexicans started speaking *Castellano* on a daily basis during the *Porfiriano Era*, though it is mixed with *Nahuatl* as Mariano Azuela asserts in his novel, *"Los De Abajo"*. Most refer to Mexican peasant language as *Rancho* Talk! Then during the post-civil war period in *México* (1921), under President Obregón, the country begins a literacy unification campaign. The ruling classes need *Castellano* in order to meet the limited goals of the reconstruction phase. Teaching Spanish nationwide therefore becomes the norm. The remaining Spanish elite that survived the civil war and now calls themselves Mexicans returned to their ancestor's practices and replaced *Nahuatl* with Spanish. The emerged language is a mixture of *Nahuatl* and Spanish, but we assume it to be Spanish. Thus most Mexicans believe themselves to be at least partially Spanish.

AN EVOLVED CULTURE

The class position of most Mexicans and Chicanos confirm we are not *mestizos*, but rather, Native Americans with a European language and religion. As previously mentioned, Mexicans violently came into contact with the Europeans and the Christians solidified their institutions in *México* through violence. Nonetheless, the arrival of the Christians can be viewed in the context of ever changing cultures and societies ranging back into and over 30,000 years and before. Human development in relation to environmental expansion can take up to millions of years. The Christians have only been in this part of the world, particularly *México*, for only 480 years. It is a short span in universal time. Prior to Christian arrival and Mexica domination of the 14th century, there had existed, the *Toltecas, Tepanecas, Teotihucanos, Olmecas, Tlatilco, Colima, Mayans* (of which there are three categories but is really not understood because the friars burnt the history books), and others to the west, north, southeast, east, and south and north. There were deserts, mountains, tropics, valley pueblos, nations, but not as tribes (a racist term to mean barbaric) and so forth.

Many pueblos had gone through vast changes in their existence, adaptation, acculturation but not destruction. One must think of the Mexicas as the pueblo, nation, which took in thousands of years of cultural and human collection. The Mexicans were both Aztecs and Olmecs of three thousand years past. The survival depended in acknowledging past knowledge with current existence all in connection to *Cihuacoatl*, mother earth and the human mother. To assume that this continuity ended with the arrival of the Christians is absurd. To say that modern *México* was born in 1521 is not to comprehend human existence for 100,000 ago. Modern Spain and the world were born through *México*, as Jack Weatherford so eloquently pinpointed in his book *Indian Givers*. Without *México*, there is no modern capitalist economy, no evolution of corporations, no expanded diet of corn, beans and potato which has expanded world populations, no pharmaceutical advancements, no U.S. Constitution, a Europe in the Dark Ages with stagnation and no age of Reason, no cotton, no flavored food, nothing. The rest of the world has benefited much more than current day Mexicans.

The Christian-Spaniards understood this longevity. That is why they attempted to destroy Mexican institutions and impose Christian ones. The Christians destroyed everything from aviaries to buildings to human life. And amidst Mexica remains, Christians rebuilt their own institutions. Clarification though, the Mexicans built those structures with Mexica knowledge and Mexica hands. By then it was too late. The Christians had won and the canon would complete the re-institutionalization.

Mexicans built thousands of churches. That was our introduction to pre-European capitalism, the real gold. Mexicans survived despite the fact that Christians cemented their stake in institutions that continue to thrive today. From children being forced to take off their fathers' shoes as if they were kings. Their only throne, 16th century disciplinary beatings, illiteracy in Spanish, dependence on

manual labor, house labor for both children and women, this is
what medieval Spain left in *México*. Though their mission was
not complete because of their notion of superiority, both in race
and class. Mexicans remained Native American because Christians' true objective was to enrich Spain. In order to do so, Mexicans could not become partially Spanish. Why? Spain would
have had to become responsible for Mexicans. Conquered people
need not a conscious colonizer to enrich the Imperial State. Simply
put, the Spaniards wanted the multiple products of riches only for
themselves.

Though I reject *mestizaje*, this does not mean that people did
not mix. Of course they did, but they were the minority rather
than the majority. Most Mexicans mixed among themselves, as is
my case. *Maayo* and *Purempecha, Otomi* and *Purempecha, Mexica* and *Tepaneca, Mixteco and Zapoteca* (though they are always
at odds, then again so are our parents), Anazazi and Zuni, Navajo
and Hopi, Chumash and Malibu. This needs to be acknowledged
first, because peoples of North America are as diverse as any
other in the world. Most are also multi-lingual, just as we Chicanos are. My partner is from *Sahuayo, Michoacán*. Though culturally different, we are both Mexicans. My fathers' family made
different tamales and spoke with an accent different than from
that of my mothers' family and they lived in the same city, *Mexicali*. Simultaneously, I do not ignore the arrival of other Europeans. Yes some Spanish, French and Germans stayed, but so did
many people from other parts of *México* and Central America.
Mexicans have always been the majority. Even today, only 10
percent of the population in *México* is European. The rest is Native American. In California, Chicanos, Mexicans, Central Americans, and Native Americans comprise the majority, 50% and
counting.

What matters is not race to Native American people, though I
do not discount race and racism, the vital emphasis is the acceptance of culture, Mexican culture. One can be of any color and be
accepted as Native American. That seems to be the case today.

This is where we need to evolve. *México* needs to rethink its *mestizo* identity because all this does is demonstrate shame. Sadly enough, the oppressed becomes the oppressor and the glorification of a *rubio* (blond person) is still the maximum honor for somebody in the Western Hemisphere. One sees more dark Mexicans in English media vis-à-vis the Spanish *noticiero* (news) where one views green eyed and white skin correspondents reporting to a majority of dark skin people.

Lets stop making apologies for being full-blooded Mexicans!

Chapter Two

The Greatest Fabrication:
la Virgen de Guadalupe

In moments of great pain, conflict or need of comfort, we have been conditioned to believe that there is an external being which will sooth the anguish. Most humans have experienced traumatizing events that may need a reason or at least they believe they do, and, or need to vent their frustration out. I know such pain, I have been there. By the age of eighteen, I had lost my father to a heart aneurysm, my mother's younger brother to a truck accident, my aunt's husband to suicide, a high school football teammate died of a heart attack right in front of me with uniform and all, my madrina, who was my second mother, and my adopted father/friend. This type of experience does lead one to search somewhere else, both physical and meta-physical.

In my search for such answers and with aging, I have come to comprehend this is life, as painful as it is. We all live to die, yet many die unexpectedly. My padrino-grandfather, who is 82 years old, has seen most of his loved ones pass on and though hurtful, comprehends these occurrences as stages in life. He still smiles and laughs. He even keeps making claims he is going to die, but he has nine lives. The same occurs to nations of people.

Mexicans suffered one of the greatest of all holocausts any people have known. We were murdered, beaten, enslaved, contaminated and spiritually, permanently-scarred by other people through the word of Christ. The metal sword came slashing through our faces, necks, chests and then a figure would do a sign of the cross with a piece of wood in his hand, then ask God to forgive us for defending ourselves. They called us pagans, idolatries, yet these same men wore a piece of wood in the shape of a cross as a necklace. With this cross they protected themselves. I never knew wood had extra-powers, other than possible shelter or warmth from an holguera.

The new army destroyed everything intentionally and then forcefully enslaved us to rebuild with the same rubble their places of worship. Catholic-Christian churches went up just as fast as the death of 20 million Mexicans. The churches were built but the souls of people knew collectively what had been there. Ecclesiastical leaders also knew, which was why they demanded Catholic Churches be constructed immediately and everywhere. Every time a cross arose on top a Christian temple, it demonstrated the power of the stake. You have all been buried now. Thus, the cross became a political symbol, both metaphysical and physical. When crosses arise on top of the Cacaxtla ruins, there is a powerful message being transmitted. The cross on top of a circular structure means, even after 480 years, we are at the top, both in life and death. To avoid memory loss and continue with the propaganda, churches with crosses still abound. The continual presence of such crosses is as political as it ever has been, both here in East Los Angeles, California and Mexico. Around East Los Angeles College, within less than a two-mile radius, there are more than four such machines. It's not just in Cholula where they seem to be in every corner. But there is a fear of a return to pass, a pass these crosses would not want to confess to.

A soother, a comforter arises, more and more so-called conversion con chingazos. The chingazos was a rush. To beat a human being senseless for not taking in the word of the señor Cristo, is a great spiritual sensual rush. The evidence proves it. People smarted up. Ni que fueramos pendejos! Si como no, Cristo es mi salvación. A forced, insincere and untruthful conversion resulted. As a teenager, I became a born-again Christian out of convenience. If I accepted, I would enjoy excursions and other activities. And I did. I went camping, weekly activities, the theme parks. Why wouldn't

I? My mother could never have provided those experiences on poverty wages. But, did I give up my past? Of course not. How could I give up my padrino, catholicism becomes partially cultural, which was not common among born-agains. I would not give up dancing as the cult demanded and I certainly could not stop lusting. These were cultural and biological characteristics of mine.

Sixteenth-century Mexicans did the same. They outwardly accepted Cristo and, the new slave names such as Jose, Maria, Gonzalo, Francisco, Antonio, Jesus, Ana, Escolastica, Saturnina, Elizabeth, Magdalena, and others, but inside their callis-homes and pueblos, they were Mixtli, Citlalli, Xochitl, Pactli, Topiltzin, and Cuautemoc. The Christians believed they were converting them, but every place of worship where a santo was positioned, it really meant a Mexica Cihuacoatl, Tonatiu, Ollin, Ehecatl, and Tonantzin. The Christians believed they had to save these souls from hell. The Mexicas understood that hell had arrived, why would they want to go to that place?

The Spanish Christians decided that the conversion of Mexicans had to become more sophisticated. There had to be an appearance of a "milagro" that had to be similar to the Mexicas. They noticed that many went to this hill they called "Tepeyac". The Mexicans went there for a pilgrimage, a reason. Probably asking why the chosen people were forsaken. The Christians observed and comprehended, "We must make a connection." A connection between ellos and los Cristianos. The plan was now how to set it up.

Bishop Juan de Zumarraga in conversation with his high priests and political leaders, discussed and decided on the pivotal point. That cerro! Everything had to be done in connection with the Mexicans' regular places of worship.

"We'll make an appearance of la virgen Maria appear like a Mexican. Una morena, plus she'll speak Mexicano, Nahuatl. She'll appear in that site of the Mexicans and we'll build upon it."

The fact that it was Juan Diego, is irrelevant. It could have been any individual. Juan Diego was the slave name for Cuauhtlatohuac (He who talks like an eagle from Cuauhtitlan.).

He supposedly returned with roses in a cloak after a few tries and there was the image of some dark virgin Maria, re-named from Arabic origin and there now exists the "most famous" Mexican female name, Guadalupe. A church was built in her honor and so were hundreds more, not necessarily in her honor."

The Christians then began the propagandistic work of making this new imposition widely accepted. The validity of this miracle must now be highly questioned because they and only they wrote history in their terms and under their penmanship. The Mexicans had no say in this time. Just as during the Chronicles, only the Spaniards were writing for their aggrandizement. Thus, the imposition begins.

Guadalupe was not comprehended nor accepted originally. Mexicans were worshipping Tonantzin, goddess of fertility. There is no account of this miracle from the Mexicans' point of view and with everything being written in Spanish, most Mexicans could neither read nor write in their language. This was the case up to less than eighty years ago. Those vestiges of Spanish illiteracy are still visible in my grandparents and many, many, many, Mexicans on both sides of the border. Moreover, the bible in the 16th century was in Latin and up until twenty-five years ago, most masses were also conducted in Latin in Mexico. What did Mexicans really comprehend? Not much other than procedures; as a child I waited for the ostia, I knew when mass would almost be over.

Second, one must remember that Judeo-Christian thought arrived only via España. Had the virgen de Guadalupe arrived before any signs of Christianity, I could accept her validity. There are no traces of this Middle Eastern/Northern African/European religion anywhere in the western hemisphere. Only the Chupacabra has flown from Puerto Rico to Mexico and that is possible because birds do fly and migrate.

As the first century under permanent slavery engulfed Mexico and in all directions, people were baptized and if the California Missions are indicative of past history, acceptance of Cristo was a logical choice. As the historical memory still lingered about Tenochtitlan, the remaining Mexicans told of the grand city and cities that they saw as young people and then their offspring told other offspring and so forth. The later generations, those into the 17th century did accept Christianity and the virgen because they were born into those institutions. They were born with the local parochial down the street, the cross in every other corner and more and more and more crosses. The image of the virgen de Guadalupe gets disseminated from priests to priests to priests to Mexican to Mexican to Mexican to Mexican and continues today to Mexicans on both sides of the border.

Catholicism is doing more than conversion. The clergy imbed and make this faith cultural. It is not just a Sunday session of fifty minutes. It is an institution of every second of every minute of every hour of every day of every week of every month of every year of every decade and of every century.

One never escaped a constant bombardment of pre-television era propaganda. Maybe the television industry learned from the Spaniards about how to force ideals into someone's psychic. Remember, under this New World order, everything is written in Castellano, Latin and not in Mexicano. How could one develop a consciousness if only through word of mouth? Oral histories. Yet oral testimony could be limited with distance, the nearby inquisition and endless propaganda. Censorship was quite the norm in colonial Mexico. Thus the Mexican becomes Catholic because of no choice and now believes in navidad, Moises, Fransisco de Assis, los reyes magos and Jerusalen. The virgen, compadrazgo, but the Mexicans add quinceñeras and even the celebration of mass on December 12th at dawn, is a substitute for the Mexican celebration of the sun god Tonatiuh. Cooptation works but only to enforce Catholicism but also from endless missionization. Mexicans fought back and a compromise was struck. The survival of Catholicism just as capitalism rests on the premise that it can recreate itself in times of great conflict. Capitalism did so in the 1930's and grew more powerful. And, so, has Christianity in Mexico.

Now after three centuries and endless candles with the image of this woman pasted on, one accepts this as normal. A lie becomes a truth after endless vocalization. If she's one of us, well let's take it as so, just as the term Indian. That description never existed until the sixteenth century but most still use it today. It is wholly inaccurate but if one says so, you are labeled a "radical, an ethnic centrist individual and a nationalist". The fact that one wants to have his identity accurately portrayed is considered irrelevant.

This image prevails and has through time, as a cultural symbol that still represents the enslaver. The image has more of a political symbol and has taken on that role primarily through men such as Hidalgo, Villa, Cesar Chavez, but also painters, on both sides of the gender realm. It's ironic La Virgen de Guadalupe can straddle both sides. The powers that be in Mexico even fired the archbishop in the mid-1990's when he also challenged it's validity. He was accused of being anti-Mexican because how could the man which gave mass under her cloak for over thirty years make such a point. Then again, many priests are not believers, though they are some of the best entrepreneurs in the world.

This political usage is in reality the true nature those in power see in her. Her usage ranges from the state of eternal mental intoxication from among the poor to the local carnicerias to the local liquor stores who don't want taggers leaving their marked space to paintings on vans, canvasses and even as good luck for the gamblers. I always thought of the image as the calendar chick from the local carnicerias to the local panaderias.

This blind devotion is problematic considering the fact that most people who believe in her are poor and the state uses that. Even with forty million people going hungry on a daily basis in Mexico and here in Los Angeles, there is still this blind trust she will save them. How many people have died crossing the border? The virgencita is incapable of doing anything because she is just a sticker. And she continues to become popular as conditions worsen.

If an individual states that "La virgen is a lie", that creates chaos for attacking the most sacred. This image has more acceptance than people's own misery. This brainwashing prohibits any political consciousness because if the church or state manipulate such an event through la virgencita, then they have the upper hand. And by maintaining this false illusion as sacrosanct, one has lost the battle of consciousness because the faith is tied into the cultural. Most Mexicans are believers in the Southwest yet, we are still the most impoverished. One can pray, though, to no avail. It is humans, wealthy ones, who control life here on earth.

Tragically when she appears in Southern California people flock. Her appearance even becomes part of the 6:00 p.m. news in English. That in itself is a major accomplishment! Normally, Chicanos can only get coverage when stereotyping is occurring. She even appeared in Lennox, one of the most dense, impoverished, Mexican reservations in Los Angeles County under the path of the Los Angeles International Airport. The commotion was so great that it almost seemed as everybody's high school reunion. There was nothing there other than a silhouette of an oblong egg. Other than that, what milagro accorded. Our poverty was not alleviated. My mother was still working as a slave, drive-by shootings were the norms and there was no hope other than going to UCLA.

She became marketable and many merchants have cashed in. As always a pimpification! News coverage made us seem like those individuals talking in plantation language of "si siñor, a sus ordenes y mande usted". This slavery has not left us and the virgen is a very intregual component of such devotion. The consequences are still more impacting when we analyze by gender:

For men, the female partner they aspire to must resemble these qualities of chastity and purity. Anything else is less. They then judge women within the usage of their vagina and nothing else. The brain is of irrelevant matter within this paradigm.

For women, to be like an entity, which never existed, is as unrealistic as prayer and equality. Women are supposed to be pure, untouched, inhuman, enduring of the worst and sympatetic to crimes committed against them.

For gays and lesbians, sorry, you are not in this equation. You will be sent to hell so they say. You can not love a man because he has a penis and you cannot love a woman because she doesn't have a penis. Where is the logic?

For artists, there are many things that can be painted, but, please, no more images of la virgen de Guadalupe. I'm all Guadaluped out!

Recently, there is a new teaching on the virgen de Guadalupe. That she must be understood within the context of Tonantzin, the goddess of fertility. That the virgen really represents Tonantzin. I can comprehend the historical clarification but why not call her Tonantzin? What is the fear? Is this another apology, just like the mestizo? The voices of conformity cannot call Mexicans what they are, Native Americans. La virgen de Guadalupe is Tonantzin, one should use her verdadero nombre! If one reaches this stage then I can lend an ear. While she continues as propaganda, I'll still think of her as the calendar chick from the local carniceria.

Chapter Three

The Myth of Machismo

As a male, I was raised with the inherent idea that I was a macho. A macho because I had *huevos, cojones (a non-Mexican term I have learned) y pelotas a Bolivian lexicon*. Biologically I was macho, but characteristically that was to be determined.

Early on, I failed in being macho. I did not live up to a *Camacho*. That name was mere coincidence. I was a *lloron*, hombres no lloran and I could never live up to my father's standards. I was not tough, though I was a child and was considered to be *muy chiquiado*. I hung on to my mother because she was caring, patient, and most important, affectionate. My father was cold, unfriendly, and not affectionate. He wanted me to be macho like him, but he was twenty-two years old and I was a three-year-old. In retrospect, what could an urban-rural transnational Mexican-Chicano Maayo peasant man provide to me? In his eyes, by me being *muy lloron*, I was not being prepared for the harshness of life. I was, by living, but I liked to cry. I still like to cry as a thirty-year-old man, it soothes internal pain. A former student of mine, a male my age stated, "Llorar is what makes a man, a macho".

Though to be called a *lloron, a maricon*, which implies at times a cry-baby, but more generally a homosexual, was psychologically catastrophic. *Pues, soy?* Because I cry and cried a lot. I could never reconcile that term though, because every time I was being called a *maricon*, I knew they were calling me a fagot. Even if fagot had a non-sexual connotation, the categorization of not living up to the accepted standard still resonated a lack of being male. In retrospect, this was also a case of a bully picking on a weaker being. My father was a young male, yet, I assure him now in his *tumba* (he died in 1980) that he could not inflict the same kind of fear because now I was comparable to him in strength. Thus, he was using what he had over me, power. His power was all-encompassing. He could forcefully defeat me. He was five times taller. He could use his only power, his strength, and he did. He used it violently towards my mother. And I internalized this anger. I took this to be a sign *of un hombre macho.*

I wanted to be the opposite. I did not want to be *macho*, it was bad enough I carried this label in my last name. I wanted to be understanding, carrying, non-violent and equal to my future partner. I wanted to hold hands, kiss in front of my future children, not control movements or be angry without reason. As I became a young man, I tried to be the opposite of the male role model I had seen for the first ten years of my life. Afterwards, the male ceased to exist. No more role models and especially not from Mexican men. Those that attempted to understand after my father died, like my mother's older brother or my father's close friend were too controlling. I had to abide by their sayings. I couldn't handle being told anything by no foreigner. My mother had the best influence on me. I joined a Christian church with positive role models, but in all honesty, I was pimping and this was a way out as a poor, teenage Chicano. Not that I didn't value them, but the self-interest was the primary reason.

I proved my manhood through sports: football, wrestling and work. But that was no different than any woman who also participated in similar events. She proved her womanhood. We both had the strength to endure. The true definition of macho: perseverance. Simultaneously, I had seen my mother endure all kinds of suffering from working in heavy machine shop employment, plus raise five boys at the same time and constantly deal with male neighbors who wanted to impose their strength over our parking space (my brothers eventually physically kicked their ass and they never bothered us again. Better yet they left the *vecindad*). My mother truly was the ultimate survival.

Thus, I had to be more like my mother and her characteristics, but also the opposite of my father. And I attempted. I believed in being a gentleman with high school females, *respetoso*, but that never got me anywhere. Better yet, females would say, "you're too nice". Later in my late twenties, I would hear, "*I need a challenge*". I was on the non-receiving end more often than not. But eventually, I met a very beautiful nice woman. We dated for over seven years, but our single difference, was I did not do things according to her style or will. When I did not abide, I would endure the wrath of a woman. When I would abide, things were smooth but at my internal expense. Eventually, I developed a secret life. One with her and another outside of her. I believed in being honest about people I met on trips while she went to her home country in South America and I to Mexico, though I never heeded my mother's advice: "*No siempre se dice la verdad*". You do not always tell the truth.

Eventually I learned to be selective. I did not want to but the fight was never worth it. I found more peace by keeping quiet versus sharing. I continuously felt there was a power struggle going on, about everything. I eventually left to move away from this type of relationship. This is not to demean her because there were many great moments, but at times, the bad outweighed the good. I noticed her mother was also a control freak and her father had divorced her mother for the same reason, as he would mention on occasions.

I then moved on, met somebody else and married her. I thought I was also running from the opposite person, though in hindsight, she was worse. My ex-wife functioned in a manner in which she wanted to have final say over every action taken. I understood consultation but, at times, one needed to trust the other person. When I did not abide even after explaining my reasons, the fight did not end until she felt tired of fighting or I eventually accepted blame. Many times, accepting blame was much easier than continuing to differ. She came to dominate many aspects of the marriage. She had final say on children, she had final say on sex, she had final say on when to install the internet and final say on what she deemed important. I then began to feel helpless. I questioned my role as a husband and felt more like a kid being scolded by his mother.

Even my ex-brother in law stated to me: "You needed to lay the rules down from the beginning." Rules! Wasn't it obvious we had to respect each other and when each asked for what they needed in the relationship, was that not enough communication? It wasn't. I then began to feel like a prisoner in my own home and had to deal with a dead bolt in my bedroom. I felt powerless and was unfaithful. The unfaithfulness was a way of obtaining a certain sense of control in my life and self-esteem. It was not correct but it was the only way to validate who I was because even in intimacy, I was made to feel inept. Outside I realized I wasn't, we had power issues I could not live with. And when I acted on what I believe was best, I was chastised for being selfish.

I then confessed to my infidelity as a way of vengeance and releasing and left humiliated, defeated but needing to start over in another life. I learned that in this relationship, I had been overcome by a "macho woman", not just a strong woman. I knew what a positive strong woman could be in my mother, but she was not controlling. I was viewed as a jerk for my infidelity, but I was solely blamed and lost many so-called friends. Though the one thing I still carry in me is my ex-brother-in-law's advice," you needed to lay down the law straight from the beginning". Maybe he was correct about being not controlled or maintaining some sense of power was the only means of survival. I left with his advice and have not deviated.

I later learned everybody attempts to control or obtain the upper hand, males and females. As long as somebody does not get *chingarred (fucked) over.* Thus, by dominating or controlling, both genders are "machos". Women are just as willing to control their partner through sex, children,and attitudes whereas men attempt to control through attitudes or even infidelity. Violence is quite common, but this is an extreme form of control.

Forced power over somebody, is violence but is not macho. And violence occurs in both intra and inter gender groups and towards children. The same Chicano father has probably fought another male and some Chicanas have fought other females. This is the most extreme, but violence is quite common in both the US and Mexico, though there are limited forms of remedies, either through law, organizations, social workers and so forth. A deconstruction of violence needs to be learned.

In my current relationship, I have applied my former brother-in-law's previous advice. I have set guidelines and so has she. As long as they are not violated, there is peace. In essence we are both being macho, though in a positive sense: two strong-willed people who respect each other and do not attempt to dominate.

Yet the dominion of machismo extends beyond just my personal relationships. They include all the Mexicanas and Chicanas I have known in my life. Better said, I have never known a weak Mexicana or Chicana woman in my life. Mi ama, mi mami, mi mama, mis tias, my partner, my ex-wife, and my ex-ex girlfriend who was Bolivian were not weak women. These were women who have controlled with their personalities and bodies.

I have explained the women I was involved in, but let's look at my grandmothers. I continuously read about how in Mexican times, prior to the arrival of the Christians, society was matriarchal. In my reality, this has never ceased. Both of my grandmothers were macho women who dominated through character, body and violence. My paternal grandmother is a Maayo from Los Mochis, Sinaloa who only stands five feet, two inches, though she ran her family of ten children with an endless influence. She was a fighter. She was married five or six times providing me with multi-ethnic grandfathers from Mexicans, to Filipinos to Anglos and back to Purempechas. She labored in the fields in the 1960s at the Coachella grape strike and in Salinas. She also raised at least six grandchildren in addition to her ten children who are now all adults.

My mami was brutal to the daughters and daughters-in-law. If I was a woman, I would not have married into that family. Poetically, she tore up my mother and the other women. My grandmother was my mother's worse enemy. Mexican mothers take on a vengeful role against their sons' new partners. At times she mounted almost a crusade type of attack, though she was not selective. Mami would lash out at my *tias,* calling them *pirujas, whores.* The *tias* left as young as fourteen and mami was not forgiving. If they divorced and wanted to return, they were not welcomed. "*Queria marido hijita, ahora chingese*", I would hear her say. The same happened with my partner's mother and grandmother.

Estas viejas no perdonaban. I believe my grandmother lightened up and was rejuvenated with the adopted grandchildren but after great losses.

Las tias were also another case. They emulated the matriarch. They attempted to behave in the same manner that in an argument, my matriarchal tia, sister of my mother, coined *La Loba,* the wolf, put a permanent stop by referring to them as having been "*criadas en un rancho, pero no entre putas*". My mother was looked down upon for being a country versus an urban girl from Mexicali. Go figure, the place is one big *rancho.* The men were generally passive and my father would not stand up to his mother or sister but would bring havoc on my mother.

In reference to my maternal grandmother, my mother and tias have this profound anger towards her for being savage. Physical violence was the norm and had they been in Calexico, my *ama* would have been arrested for child abuse. My grandfather, on the other hand, was passive and wouldn't challenge her. Furthermore, I learned through my sister that my ama refused to have sex with my grandfather after the birth of their last daughter in 1960. He was crying to her that my sister, encouraged him to have sought out another woman. I was also introduced to a beating ala my ama levied upon my sister and I'm still traumatized. Thus, we see continuous power struggles ensuing from the matriarch towards other people, especially women. My ama was also known to have used corporal punishment on her eighteen-year-old son in the mid-1970s. He tragically died in an accident, and I bet she now wishes she had not.

My *tia, la loba*, my mother's sister has always been a brute: First with her daughter, (favored her son) and then towards my brothers, but my teenage years were spent fighting her and I never backed down. Now, maybe because of age, she is careful because we still accept her but underneath her veil, she's a raging bull. Prior to the death of her husband, she was known to use a wooden spoon on him, but in the early years, she also endured his violent wrath. Thus, both males and females behave in a similar way because power is being played out.

Even my mother, who has taken her share of lumps, has not been immune. One would think because she has suffered, she would change her paradigm. She acted no different than any of my grandmothers towards the daughters or daughters-in-law. As an example, my mother did not like my ex-wife and those differences played themselves out. I did not know that side of my mother. She was brutal and unsupportive and that weighed on me. Eventually, when I divorced, my mother was quite happy, though I have noticed that she does not act that way towards the new women in our lives (my brothers). Now she is political. She might not like a certain person, but she keeps her opinion to herself. Thus she continues to be a matriarchal macho, though she states, "My love is unconditional, I only want the best for you." And she has taught us not to trust women and with men it's a given, never trust no one. She further states, "take a look at those women who take advantage of their *maridos* and those who screw the father over through child support. Do the courts assist fathers versus mothers? My experience has seen, that fathers are guilty then have to prove their worth over laws that automatically favor mothers."

Lastly, this is not a specific case visible only in my surroundings. My ex-wifes' family consisted of seven sisters and two brothers. All the women were more macho than the husbands, except for a Sicilian. The difference with me was I couldn't handle being controlled or having to become passive.

The understanding here is that machismo is much more complexed than a male dominating the household, because that is rarely the case. Most women in Mexican households govern the house. What exists are people vying for power both directly and indirectly over each other. When it's men, it is called machismo; when it's women, they are strong-willed. There cannot exist a double standard, because both controlling genders are erroneous. Humans need to be given the maximum freedom to be themselves whether a partner or child.

Both groups need to be aware of power and must be conscious to not exploit such virtue, otherwise chaos will reign. As for me, having the last name of Camacho is more than enough machismo in me. Remember, macho means to persevere, not exploit.

Chapter Four

The Pimpification of Mexico's Export Labor Class: Mexican Workers in the U.S. are Prostituted for Mexico's Elite

ANNUAL REMITTANCES OF SIX BILLION DOLLARS!

Mexican workers: women, men and children annually contribute to towns, such as Jerez, Jiquilpan or Penjamo. For years, oil and tourism have ranked as two of the highest capital grossing industries in all of Mexico, though this has required great capital investment. Either industry requires great infrastructure. Remittances must be viewed as an equal economic machine to that of oil and tourism, though exporting workers is much easier. Generally, the Mexican elite has not invested in education other than beyond sixth grade or even la *secundaria*. Visit the *primarias* in Mexicali with an outhouse and no air-conditioning in the summer. "International" Mexican workers do not require much capital investment, other than paved roads to the north from *el golfo de Mexico to Tijuana* and many points in between and not so subsidized bus fairs on *Norte de Sonora, Tres Estrellas* or *Omnius de Mexico*. I have never seen the *nouvou riche* buses I have traveled on through central Mexico heading north. Those are used for tourists.

When you head north either as a rite of passage or as a new employee, you are introduced to the harshness of the new world in Sonora, the desperateness of the Baja California mountain range and the freeway caution signs. If you have gotten this far, you are lucky. Then you are ready to be enslaved for any industry. Agriculture, garment, cook, busboy, carwash, housecleaning, room service, construction, gardening and wherever desperateness leads one to.Yet let's back up!

La frontera! Crossing this real imaginary line can be life-threatening. Some years back as I traveled through Cheran, Michocan, I was told this is the town were the mother, *una madrecita,* lost her three sons being chased by the *migra*, the Death Squad for American corporations and Mexican elite. The van was chased and was forced to crash somewhere on highway 15. Would three crosses be permitted to be placed? Would it matter? Could la virgencita obtain a piece of paper for those impoverished Mexicans, originally Purempechas? I felt a chill through my spinal soul. How could a mother bury three sons at the same time? Young men, who did not leave their seeds. Cheated out of life. I wanted out of Cheran because the pain was too unimaginable. Later this year, some people froze to death up on the mountains near San Jacinto and others have died in the desert north of El Centro, my birthplace. Did they have to die? Is this how the Mexican elite and American corporations ensure commitment? Why doesn't there exist a human pact? Obviously this is the only way to docile this labor force. A piece of paper is what lives are worth.

Yet, do Mexican elite, whether business people, singers, athletes or even visiting university professors risk such dangers? No, they are given unlimited visas. They come and go at will. No danger to their lives. No thirty-five hour bus ride. No not showering for two days. No toilet paper in their nylon bags. They just pay for their airplane tickets and are in Los Angeles or Houston with no delays. The Mexican rich come, splurge, and return to Mexico showing off their new recent acquisitions, while many poor Mexicans consume hunger. I remember 1983 when my sister's refrigerator did not have food. *Vacio. No nos fiaban carne en el abarrotes.* No credit for *pellejo!* The inter-lining of flesh from the fur. The fur becomes shoes or bags, the meat Mexicans eat as delicatessen, though you know it's near cannibalism. As you bite the meat, the nerve still twigs in-between your teeth. We only ate frijoles, though my brother-in-law worked for *La Comision Federal de Electricida en el Cerro Prieto.* In 1999, I asked my sister about how in 1983 we could not afford meat and my brother-in-law insisted, *"Todavia no podemos".* Meat is a privilege. Throughout Mexican California, *carnicerias* are overly shopped. Carnicerias are the most hip places. Even in Solvang, when on a camping trip with my students, they found a carniceria, with the meat marinated. It was segregated, away from the out of place architecture, but it reassured what was once hard to obtain is obtainable even if within the limitations in Los Angeles.

Thus most Mexicans suffer in their place of birth and are forced out. Would they have it this way? Would their lives be as enriched had they never left their pueblo, ciudad or rancheria? They would have traveled but not to suffer, as I have lived myself. Then, if hunger is a way of life for many and others do not suffer, why do Mexican workers subsidize them? Why do Mexican workers make the Mexican elite get off so easy? Is *la patria,* as many say, that valuable? I hated Lennox because of the immense poverty and segregation I had to live through and still hate Los Angeles, California, the United States of America and Mexico in all its entirety.

Many Mexicans die and the Mexican elite are not held accountable for their crimes committed to my mother, or somebody's father, or sister or brother and so forth. Yes, the Mexican government cries wolf, the Mexican consuls pretend to be local ambassadors but go to the *consulado* and see how one is treated like an *humilde campesino,* a peon who gets shuffled like a dice. All to return to the land, in reality to those who would not provide the means for sustenance. People clamor to return to the tierra querida, though I once heard somebody say, *"Yo soy fiel a la tierra que me da de comer".* One is faithful to the lesser of two evils. Some choice!

Criminal charges need to be brought upon those individuals in Mexican society who control the purse, whether internal and

external. During the early 1980's, Mexican capital flight was
quick to arrive to La Jolla and Houston. The elites have placed
many on the *Trail of Tears* to the north, enough die and others
make it to the enslavement centers. One is humiliated in the place
of work. No one talks to Mexican busboys, they are invisible. Or
people like them to be. Mexicans can wipe the leftovers though
they may not serve them. There is a better tip if the host or
waiter/tress is "American". Discrimination and a hierarchy in the
place of eatery.

The owner of the hairstyling salon whether Chinese or Middle
Eastern can fully humiliate a Mexican woman; in reality he is
fucking her with shame. If the Mexican woman isn't being
fucked with shame, she might be getting fucked in another place.
I have always wondered if my mother as a seventeen-year old
housekeeper in Pacific Palisades wasn't fucked. *Se la habran
chingado!* She never talks about this place, maybe I don't want
to hear.

The *costureros*, those that sew. I remember the faces of a
Honduran nineteen-year-old, a forty-something Mexican man
aged with wrinkles and ashamed, never to wear the Guess blazer
he sewed, the women with their headphones and their repetitive
motion, waiting for those breaks to expedite the workday. I remember a cook, a friend of the family who is permanently
greased. His hands have lost their natural oils, they are now
Criscoed. His whole body resonates every flavor from twenty
years' of cooking.

My mother would arrive sometime after 4:00 PM and would sit
dead, with her head arched up and hands slopped down. I can still
see her pain twenty years later. The machine shop took away her
best years, the airline kitchen her natural body sleep. Now by
9:00 PM, she aches from having to sleep. Fuck both countries!
This is the same for millions. If their earnings are slaved, what do
many do? They send a certain amount to their *padrote.*

A pimp! A pimp never does anything. He claims to have provided clients, but biology works that out. How can someone claim
credit for having done no tasks?

The Mexican elite with their puppeteers, the government, are the *alcahuetes*. The Madame is both female and male.

Through the disguise of a false sense of patria and the motherland, plus loved ones, one feels obligated to send back. Many remit money to pueblos that normally would not receive outside income. Yet, the Mexican elites do nothing to remedy such a situation. They place this responsibility on the impoverished and indirectly encourage them to migrate. They claim constitutionally, that it is unlawful for Mexicans to not leave though they do nothing at facilitating even if they are providing false documentations to save their fellow country people from dying. A local passport would do great to save people. Many would say that is illegal, though no Mexican town is willing to return money they have accepted for doing nothing. The pimp collects.

Through sweat and humiliation, millions of Mexicans send a percentage, as small as it might be. It becomes significant enough to equate from four to six billion dollars per year. Towns have streets paved, ambulances bought, churches built (why?), homes built that generates the whole construction industry from simple things such as faucets and mirrors to doors to paint. But what do the Mexican elite do in return? Do they alleviate hunger? Do they provide better wages? Are towns assisted in helping the older folks? Do they provide sanitary conditions? I still use an outhouse in Mexicali.

Thus, the *padrote* collects billions for doing nothing. Why would the Mexican elite ever want to alter an economic machine that requires little capital investment with a return equating that of the top two industries? Six billion dollars for doing nothing! What a privilege for the privileged. What a give away from those in need. Yet Mexicans continue giving away and subsidizing. Under this paradigm, nothing will ever change. And thousands more will risks themselves and many will also die in the winters and summers of the Sonoran desert. Their resting place will be los jardines del desierto.

To add insult to injury, many Mexicans living in the United States who send monthly money to loved ones, paying annual property taxes and so forth, are not even allowed to participate in the political process. But does the Mexican crust return the money people send?

In this last decade, one has seen Mexican politicians making their way up to California and campaigning for monetary and moral support, whatever the party. Obviously, people comprehend a vital exists, which is to maintain that linkage between here and there, primarily through dollars but disguised as the patria, lo cultural. The Mexican national soccer team, la virgen on tour, endless similar banda groups and through novellas and other Televisa programs. In my opinion this is precisely where the impact can be felt.

ALTERATIONS

I once heard we needed to vote with our wallet. Therefore, I now propose we protest with our wallet. Why should Mexicans in the states subsidize the Mexican State?

The one way to alter is to curtail remittances:

1. Send only for elderly needs, primarily food and medicine (unless they want to migrate to the U.S. with you)
2. Maintain the family united by bringing them to the United States. Family reunification is the healthiest scenario for all children, wives, husbands and even grandparents.
3. Stop living in two places. All investments should be for one's primary residence here in the states (my family built a home in Mexicali except for my grandparents living in it, the house was empty for certain years until my sister moved in).
4. Mexican immigrants, you are never going to return because your children have been Chicanoized. *Paren de atormentarlos.*

If the Mexican elite wants to assist let them pay for it. Why should the most impoverished be asked to solve historical issues?

Now this doesn't mean I'm unrealistic or anti-Mexican, but neither should we continue to be indirectly forced through patriotisms, guilt, Catholicism or any other Mexicanness because I recommend we protest the injustice to working people on both sides of the borders.

Let's not sugarcoat a false reality. Mexican workers are pimped by the Mexican millionaires; it's about time the abuse stops.

Chapter Five

The False Illusion
of the Chicano/Mexicano Family

As a young adult, I would hear from well-intended people, the positive attributes of Mexican L.A. The arrival of the Mexican family reintroduces the notion of family to America. My history professor at El Camino College would praise us because we-Mexicans-frequented each other, unlike Anglos who only visited each other every thirty years. I felt good! I know why they said it. They were progressive and wanted to alleviate the Mexican on-slaught. We were becoming the new majority through large families, either by birth or migration and whites had to adjust. Mexicans could reunite the lost America! I respected that opinion but that wasn't what I had been raised to believe.

Were we Mexicans happy because of large families? I define large families not in how many children each woman had, rather, the connection between a nuclear family and the extended family or kinship: grandparents, aunts, uncles, cousins, second cousins and beyond.

My definition of family is the following: mother and siblings (one sister and four brothers). Other definitions include, father (biological or adoptive father), mother and siblings or on rare oc-casions, father-children and no mother. Personally, I have no chil-dren, though I have been married. I do not define this marriage as a family because the relationship may end and a new one begins. Not until I have children with that special person, will I consider myself to have started my own nuclear family. Then my immediate family becomes secondary, as was demonstrated by my mother. Nonetheless, as adult siblings, we are linked by memories, trials and tribulations. As we wonder off, if there is failure, we are always welcomed back. But as adults, relationships do matter and reach a non-competitive parity. Though the love exists, it is not conditional unlike with our mother. And that is fine. My mother has instilled, that we will have multiple partners. The key is to be respectful to yourself, therefore to one's partner and diligent to one's own children, if we have them (four out of five males in this family have no children including myself; my sister has two teenagers).

Lastly, my father died twenty years ago, thus my mother was both, female and male simultaneously.

The extended family; What did it mean? My experience and from what I have observed from friends depends on the upbringing. My mother believes due to her upbringing in this rancho outside of Mexicali, southeastern California, that family included third cousins. The real reason was that they were all raised together as neighbors. The memory bonds them in youth though not in adulthood. As a teenager during our stays in Mexicali, she would introduce me to this cousin of hers and so forth and so forth. I had no connection! I would tell her as an adult, just because they are your relatives, this does not mean they are mine, she would hiss away!

On another occasion, she introduces me to her oldest cousin, encourages me to stay with her family and never tells me why this cousin was distant. Incest! My tia (aunt) became a new addition of the family though if I had met any of her daughters at a club, I might have had sex with any one of them.

I learned that the more I interacted with certain cousins, the more I tended to think of them as family, versus, other cousins whom I never saw. A newly introduced relative was a brief conversation.

From the large family of my father, nine siblings and thirty cousins, I learned we did not want to associate with them. Part of the problem originated in the first conflict that I believe is universal. *The suegra!* Most mother-in-laws do not truly welcome a new wife or new husband. They see them as competition and never good enough. My mother suffered endless trauma from my paternal grandmother, a Mayo native from Sinaloa, who looked hypocritically at my mother because she had had a daughter from another man. Though my own grandmother had been married at least five times. (All my tias also suffered from an imposing suegra)! Oddly, the daughters (the *cuñadas*) of the imposing matriarch behaved just as brutal. My father's sisters thought the worst of my mother. There was endless trauma about control, manipulation and at times unmet expectations. For example, my tia would drop off her children and we had to deal with their habits, mannerisms and at times their attitudes. We use to have major altercations with our cousins that one broke out onto the street. I rarely wanted to assemble with them because I thought myself superior. Arrogant was how my mother raised us because most of them were *maleandros*, hoodlums, ghetto.

I honestly liked the fact we were generally two hundred miles away. Most of them lived in El Centro, California, north of Mexicali, Baja California. Even in the year of my father's death, there had been trauma with his younger brother because my father refused to loan him money. My father died without them talking. My father's death meant the close to total separation from that side of the family. Two additional members have died and we were never notified. To not be notified for a Mexican funeral is to be excommunicated.

My mother's side was interesting because my grandparents did not give drama to my father. As a matter of fact, they had a mutual respect. The trauma in this family came from within the siblings. My mother in her quirky personality would differ from my tia (La loba(female wolf) was her nickname) who lived near by and would on occasions not talk for a year. Ironically, my father and her husband were the best of friends, but they rationalized that if the sisters fought, they would have to work it out on their own terms. My mother would live through periods of peace then

experience mean spirited fights. For example, once they with each
eldest daughter had a negative fight-verbal in front of my grandmother and I walked into it with an ex-girlfriend not knowing
what occurred. It was embarrassing plus frustrating because it
seemed life would never change.

Another tia was stealing as much as possible from my grandparents and my mother's eldest brother was a self-centered pri-
mogeniture. He has always been self-centered and has never
given a damn about his mother and father. He also ran out on his
family. Better yet, he had two families at the same time, infants
born days apart. How many Mexican fathers have not fathered
children on the side? He was not friendly to my brothers and me
at a time we longed for a male father figure. Maybe it was unfair
to ask of him! I just learned to keep my distance from everybody.
What would I want from them? I had to make my own family.
And I did.

I think back to what my teachers would say excitedly about
Mexican families, they are family oriented. The reality was much
more complicated. Mexican families to me were a burden. Many
times I longed to be alone, just my mother and siblings and quite
often we were until somebody needed a place to stay. The stay
was always uncomfortable because we didn't have enough space,
but we couldn't say no!

Were Mexican families that beneficial? I believe it is best to
look at the conditions one existed in, to comprehend the time and
space and the relation to Los Angeles. I further believe the coming together of Mexican families in Los Angeles had more to do
with need because of the intense loneliness, social and economic
limitations.

Most Mexican families I have come across seem to have two
camps, or two divisions and quite frequently more. When we
travel to Mexicali, we always come across that my two tias have
not visited each other in months, though they live three miles
away. Even with the fact that one tia takes care of my grandmother who is almost bedridden. This is also generational; my
grandfather who is 85 year-old does not visit his 83 year-old sis-

ter because neither family takes them, though they live five miles away (Both of them passed away on December 10th and December 23rd of 2002; both preferred to jointly continue their path in the next dream). Why? They do not need assistance from each other. With the economic limitations each Mexican family faces, fleeing is one way of saving for one self, especially if one is a little better off. I saw the same scenario in Michoacan, Durango and Coahuila. The fear of death brings people in for a short lapse of time and then everybody returns to their routines.

The reason why children are here is best to comprehend the living conditions. Oddly, most people born in rural towns came from a large family because the old man needed inexpensive field help. Natural reproduction was the most feasible. Families were having seven or eight children because the rancho could survive with all the help available. When they became a burden and required more resources, then the children were set upon paths of migration and off to the city or the states they came. When the father had also migrated, the eldest children would whether son or daughter take his role. Most children would escape through marriage as a hope for a new life. Sadly, they are always for the worst. Even when there were large families, the decision to have more children had to do with securing natural social security. When one became an *anciano*, their hope of survival rested upon any of their children. The more they had, the more choices there existed. To conclude that these people had no comprehension of reproductive methods is erroneous. Their knowledge was sufficient for survival and in congruent with world knowledge for its time, whether the 1950's, 1960's or present. This is visible today even in Mexico. Because Mexicans have become urbanized, most families now only have two to three children.

Second, many parents also had children because nature kicked in. The urge to have sex, as is natural became the norm. One quite frequently sees many young parents with older children. Education being limited with abortion illegal or taboo resulted in children having children. Quite often, the parental skills of the peasantry whether urban or rural, was no more than tending to the herd. A child had to mature on both sides of the border depending on the need, either as a field or house servant or translator, then being scolded about not adequately translating. Discipline was corporal. The way a hog was castrated equated the intensity of the *paliza*. This is also generational! My mother has the same anger towards her mother and my former wife to both her parents. If both of them could, the inner anger would result in their shooting the parents, though human decency has prevailed. My mother and ex-wife through children and herself, respectively. Many men have had a similar experience. My friend Marcos Ramos quite frequently refers to his father by his first name, Leandro *con corage*! The lack of parental skills among the peasantry has major repercussions down the years. These children go through life traumatized, in need of care, love, affection and anger up to adults and as parents. I would never advocate elitist programs, but parental classes would suffice. And because these same child parents started life so young, they also feel unfulfilled.

Thus the reason to have children does not truly fall within the current paradigm to cherish, rather for a need or accident. Yet, in America, one could argue, that the opposite has occurred. Now there exists a dieing out of the middle class family, even for Chicanos. The more one ascends, the less children people have.

And the more families have, the less they need of each other. Even large families that have migrated, they do not frequent each other because they do not need anything, other than occasional hellos.

Mexican families leave a lot to be said about their affectiveness and effectiveness. Are they that positive? Maybe. Do they bring out the best in humans? Maybe. Do they stay together because of limited choices, sadly yes and what about the nuclear family?

There is no such definition of a nuclear family as is portrayed. Apart from much trauma, many Mexican-Chicano kids grow up fatherless, as was my case. My father sadly died of a heart aneurysm, but there are countless others whose *papa*, ran away, as two of my uncles did. I find myself being a surrogate father to many students because they have none and they talk about their father through pain. They live with a vacuum, a universal endless blackhole that has no ending. Tragically, they follow the same pattern. They have children and also do not raise them. Quite often, the women use the children as politics, but many mothers are also just abandoned. Thus we have scenarios were families with fathers or without fathers and mothers or without mothers are having a negative effect on children as they are growing up. Parents can generally also be our worst enemies: One parent charges for rent and food to him even though he might be unemployed, while another gets kicked out because she tells her to stop drinking and calls the cops on her. Now this is not applicable to all, but it does have merit with others. Sadly enough, many of us come from the peasantry and only through conscious efforts via education and de-programming the paradigm of Catholic peasantry will many children have hope. Lastly, parents should not be glorified nor godified because they were the sperm or egg donors. That was easy. It was penetration, timing and release. Their glorification should come from their deeds and love can only be described as a verb. This is not unchangeable though, there are models one can learn from and must be spiritually (Non-Christian based definition) willingly, otherwise, it cannot succeed.

Creation through friendships! Amistad can be a vital tool even through compadrazgo (God parents) even if non-Catholic.

Learn to argue. Dialoging is vital but with a clear exit.
Child development comprehension.
Affection.
No glorification of anyone.
Say I love you everyday.
Never give up.

I appreciate the good intentions of my past professor, but Mexican families are quite complexed creatures that have been shaped through history and socialization. It is up to us to positively alter this institution.

P.S. There is another unspoken theme I sporadically mentioned that needs to be talked about. Incest, sexual abuse and interbreeding!

Incest is a quite common occurrence of sexual abuse by an adult, primarily male (occasionally female) as youth and adults, towards a child, both girls and boys. To talk about incest is beyond a taboo. One could argue that God does not exist, though, to talk about having been molested by somebody, particularly a family member is one of the darkest secrets many of us carry.

As a child, I had heard that incest occurred on both of my parent's side of the families. On my mother's side, her eldest cousin, a female had been sexual with her father supposedly for years. I never understood why the old man was not liked, though we all acted as if nothing had occurred until I overheard my mother's tia mention when her husband went "para alla" for fifteen years. I asked where, and both of them kept saying "para alla" (Over there). After I stayed with this female cousin of my mother during the summer of 1983, with her children a few years older than me, my sister informed me of the incest.

The "para alla" had been a fifteen-year prison sentence for my mother's uncle. He had been found guilty of sexual molestation of his eldest daughter. My sister proved her point when she asked me if I remembered a mentally handicap male who could not talk, walk upright, much less use his hands. Literally, his hands were bent downward and his feet were turned inward and pigeon toed. I remember him with black and grungy facial hair. His beard was that of an individual who was not consistently shaven. This *tia* of my mother lived in the next lot from my grandparent's home in the Colonia Santa Cecilia in Mexicali, Baja California. As children we would play in both lots and I would see him meander about. When we would get close to each other, we would be frightened by his appearance. He would try to talk and we would run from him. Little did I know until my sister told me who he was, he was the end product of this incestual relationship. He died sometime in late 1978–79. I vaguely remember hearing from one of my *tias'* in Inglewood that he had died. Nobody was notified.

My grandfather until his death did not talk to his eldest niece because according to my sister, she never put a stop to it. "It was one thing for her father to abuse her because of strength but for the sex to continue had to do with her enjoying it". The offspring ironically was taken care by the grandmother and not the daughter nor the father. Apparently, my mother's uncle went to prison from the early 1960's to sometime around 1975–76. The daughter married in the early 1960s, moved to an ejido (ranch communities), almost thirty miles away. When I stayed with her family, I could not understand why I had not met this woman and her family. She endlessly dodged my naïve questioning. She even mentioned she had been at my father's funeral but all relatives of my mother made sure to introduce themselves to us.

I believe the real pain was for my mother's tia who had to live through the years of both sexual and physical abuse. Then to have taken care of this mentally handicap child and be reminded of how this came to be must have been profoundly humiliating and mocking. Literally, she lived with her *cruz*. The original cross-burden we all carry according to Catholicism. This demonstrated great character in her, as both a woman and mother. Sadly, this came on the heels of another death to a son named Geronimo who had been mauled to death in a tractor accident that occurred sometime in the mid 1950's. My *tia Beva,* and him upon returning from *la primaria* (elementary school), would jump on the back of a tracker that would pull a flat, metal, steel poked soil turner. The tractor would pull this up and down the fields to turn the soil and prepare for sowing. Geronimo lost his balance forward and the flat metal soil turner mauled him to death. He survived for about twelve hours but died from the punctured wounds. He was buried soon after. It seemed as if my mother's *tia's* life collapsed around her.

The eldest daughter started her own family as an outcast, the father returned from prison only to return to his mocked wife. Both live with the secret pains of having committed some of the most horrendous acts towards any individual. The eldest daughter and her parents do visit each other, even when the old man is

around, though most of the time it is secretive. *Se tratan como si
nada* (As if anything ever happened)!

To not exclude my father's side of the family, the
Sinaloenses also had an incest scenario. Here the eldest brother
abused one of the middle sisters and according to my mother,
when she got married in the mid 1970's, her husband complained about her abuse and not being able to marry in a white
dress. Such hypocrisy! No legal action was taken against my
uncle because he denied it. My grandmother just accepted the
accusations, both my tio and tia where never in the same family gathering. This older uncle was an alcoholic (had to be, because he labored for thirty-years in the lettuce fields of Salinas
and Imperial Valley) had also been incarcerated from of a self-
defense fight in which he killed the other man. The other person tried to hit him with a cue stick and in return he struck him
with a brick. This man had major issues with life: starting with
being Mexican in the U.S., reinforced by back-breaking manual
labor, love gone awry, the failure of limited choices. He even
had his U.S. residency taken away. According to my grandmother, he was the only son whom she could count on, though
he might have been a drunk or killer. In 2000, he was just killed
by a drunk driver as he stood inside his fence in Mexicali. He
had worked for over thirty-five years as a farm-worker throughout California and was deported under the Clinton immigration
and felony laws. He would rather give up his green card versus
being incarcerated for years. Maybe death did liberate him
from his years of hell on earth.

This act of incest is much more prevalent though. In a course
discussion about a story called ***Macario*** by Juan Rulfo, we discussed sexual abuse and as I asked how many had lived through
such experience, at least half of the thirty-five students raised
their hands including many men. Many men stated that as children they had been sexually abused by an older male, female or
other boy. Some were teary-eyed about such situation because
it reminded them of the pain they had gone through. Women

cried because they would recollect telling their mothers and being ignored or even being blamed. The greater pain seemed to have come from being ignored by the mother versus the actual act. This pattern went on for three to four years and who knows how long for those that were intimidated to speak up. The discussion seemed to revolve around how Mexican society intentionally hides this heinous act against the indefensible. I believe that the taboos socialized by the Catholic Church and the ruling class makes this abuse all the more possible. The rational being if society cannot openly talk about sex as a natural occurrence, it is then quite easy to hide or disguise incest or sexual abuse. I saw this pattern for over three years through each Mexican literature course.

Tragically, many Chicana friends have gone through sexual abuse, either as a child, teenager or even as adults. This has been brought to light through conversation, though I do not believe this is exclusive to Chicanas. I have known European-American middle class women; one whose father was an attorney in the department of labor during the Kennedy administration, another whose father was a Christian missionary in Africa, the daughter of fisherman from Hawaii and lastly a woman I met on a Christian missionary trip to Sonora. All females had been sexually abused by a father, and brother, father (a minister), ex-boyfriend and an older brother. I was scared to death because this was the first thing coming out of their mouth. I was dealing with issues way beyond my control. In either case, I did not know how to deal with such scenario other than to listen. Most had sought counseling but that was their *cruz* to carry.

Many Chicanas tragically have also been sexually abused by an uncle, older cousin, older brother, the father, grandfather and female cousins. Upon listening to all of this, being human makes you question if there exists any human decency. Animals are much more caring and affectionate than any human being. Beast is a more appropriate term for us.

I recommended the following to students:

Seek counseling
Rape Hotlines
Call the police
Be careful of younger children with older relatives
Trust no one

Lastly, southern white folks are continuously the mock of in-breeding jokes. Though when one closely examines Mexican families, especially *Rancho Folks or Urban Persinados,* you learn that many are some how related. As a teenager, I went to a wedding in Durango and got a kick out of my friend's new sister in law referring to his mother as *tia.* Though they were like third-cousins and it did not really matter. Simultaneously, my friend's other sister had fallen infatuated with her first cousin and even dated for some time. I was even a counselor. I had no idea other than to say to myself, "I guess if I had a *prima* like you, I would do the same". The oldest brother of the male cousin at a *carne asada* would stare at his female cousin and then hiss to me to not miss out on her figure. The tight jean was considered a major attraction. They dated as best they could, but the male cousin could never openly come out. The female had more *huevos* because she confronted her mother, while I was a good listener. She eventually gave up hope on him and moved on. Last I heard, they rarely saw each other.

On another occasion, I came across former students sharing with me how their grandparents were third cousins and so forth. Others would say that their male cousins would "hit up on them" when on vacation to places such as Michoacan, Jalisco or Zacatecas. Somehow, I associate Zacatecas as the *inbreeding capital of Mexico* because this agricultural state with the endless pueblos and ranchos sends thousands of migrants to the United States and has done so for over a century. Many of these people had limited choices because of the smallness of ranchos and the strictness of the parents. The only ones they could associate with were cousins and because of the deep belief in "family-blood related" as a natural immunity, *manosiadas* (touching) occurred. This also happens in Los Angeles. A male cousin arrives in his prime and stays with his uncle who happens to have five daughters that even the handicap (physically only) seduces jointly as occurred with my first wife's sister. Another tia allows a distant cousin to live with them, only to find out that a year later, he has eloped (the traditional Mexican wedding) with one of her daughters.

This is not only a male led scenario, it includes both genders; young *tias* have been known to seduce the near age nephews or older female cousins with young boys. I once heard a *dicho" despues de primos hermanos, todo vale"*. After first cousins, everything else is fair game. A distant female cousin willingly seduced my younger brother. He was the butt of all jokes even by my grandfather. A male cousin was pursued by a fourth female cousin openly and even in front of her boyfriend. They all grew up together, went to the movies as a group and would talk continuously. At parties, she ignored her boyfriend while never losing my male cousin. In all honesty, they were distant cousins of my grandfather, but because our parents had been together, they saw themselves as siblings. Even my grandfather would tell my cousin, *"junta te con ella, son parientes alejados"*. My cousin refused and she got tired of waiting.

My second to youngest brother in his summer escapes as a twelve-year-old would talk about a sixteen-year-old daughter of my mother's cousin showing her nude body to him. His excitement was endless in his story telling form.

I truly believe this is an accepted societal norm, though all societies have had this problem from the ruling classes of Europe on down. The ruling classes thought themselves superior and the poor having limited choices. In some instances, as is visible in some Mexican films about the conquest; incest was a way of survival from the European onslaught. Thus the reasons are extremely complex. The reality though is that country folks in the American South live under similar social and economic circumstances that country folks in Mexico live through. When the

country folks in Mexico become urban peasants, a similar segregation occurs, thus inbreeding becomes an alternative. When
incest and sexual abuse prevails, one has crossed the line that
must be mitigated because there are long life repercussions.
Legislation and a non-acceptance by people themselves will
only serve as the intended deterrence. Lastly, the legalization of
brothels might be the answer as evidence indicates in the state
of Nevada where the rates of sexual abuse by adults towards
children are much lower than California.

Chapter Six

The Generation Divide: Chicano Movement Armchair Revolutionaries Wage War On New Bucks

Consistently and continuously, one hears endless examples of discrimination towards people of a certain age. We all understand this certain age to be that of maybe fifty and above. And that is the truth, however in certain industries such as where manual labor is highly in demand; construction, police (cut off age exists) and even in sales because of appearance. Yet, other industries such as agriculture, hotel, housekeeping, gardening and garments could care less of the worker's age as long as they are productive. If these industries could, they would utilize child labor as agriculture does in America.

Nonetheless, when legislation was written to protect against age discrimination, it was done so on the basis of older people being replaced by younger ones. Thus the Equal Employment Opportunities Commission salivates on claims made by older people and will attempt to remedy such situations. Yet, if a young person claims the same discrimination in reverse, to be discriminated because one is young, it is of no validity. A young 26-year-old person who enters a profession where the average age is 54 such as in most institutions of higher education, and is not rehired or granted tenure because he is "young, arrogant and in their words defiant of authority", has no legal remedy. None! Just as children have none, neither do young adults.

This has been my life existence at two institutions, Compton and East Los Angeles College, but other friends who also teach, have had a similar experience. At Compton College, it was worse, I was a Brown token for a primarily Black administration with an older white and Black faculty. Chicano issues were relegated to ESL and there the few Chicanos believed they were the lords. If nothing went through them, one was ostracized. It was odd being a Brown token, literally, because the college was on academic probation, yet as soon as the academic reprimand ended and the president who hired me was returned to the classroom, I was terminated. I had seen the writing on the wall, though I was able to stay adjunct after donating to a campaign. I was aggressive and "green" as was mentioned in the president's council on occasions. Racism with age discrimination was too much, so I left. I was the lowest paid administrator by at least ten thousand dollars and never received a raise during the two years there.

Then I went to East Los Angeles College because I had been a positive instructor and was intentionally hired because I was young and experienced both in administration and with academia, I had two master's and two bachelors. I was even considered college president material according to one colleague but I was too restless. Restless in the sense that I wanted to incorporate my recent memory of academia from Urban Planning and Latin American Studies. I wanted to create curricula that competed even with four-year institutions. I was offered the position of department chair but I turned it down and suggested that the lone female become chair instead. I then became evening chair and was given wide latitude, so I thought.

I spent the first summer decorating my wall with pictures of ruins from Latin America accumulated through my years of travel and I wrote curricula that would enhance Chicano Studies and the college as a whole. First mistake. I did not know that departments functioned as kingdoms, though in being a novice, I approached the Social Science department. At ELAC, Chicano Studies and Social Science are two independent departments, based on historical struggles in the eastside from the sixties and early seventies.

Oddly, if this department were not located at East Los Angeles College, Chicano Studies would not exist. The other departments are quite anti-Chicano and so are the older instructors in the department. It's affirmative action! This is visible through their actions and students' comments. Certain faculty pray for some of them to retire, others are just buying time, another had left for eight years and has been trying to leave to athletics. Looks like he will be the next athletic director. And the last faculty does not want to work beyond three hours per day yet makes no connection with students. She continuously complains about the low academic level of ELAC students. And this complaint came from the senior and most active member of Chicano Studies who believes the department died years ago.

Thus history matters. If you were not part of the *moimento (An old Chicano I knew could not pronounce movimiento)* you haven't paid your dues. In my case I would just bite my lip and would continue to propose new courses and from incomprehension, approached the social science department. Little did I know, nor truly comprehended, some faculty members in Social Science had left years before and they were still carrying a grudge from the early eighties. Because I came from an interdisciplinary Master's program, a joint course with social science seemed logical, yet was instantly rebuffed. I learned that everything was personal. I presented the following courses:

Central Americans: The New Chicanos
Environmental Problems in the Chicano Community
The Iberian Influence on the Chicano People
Chicano Gangs in Southern California

A pandora's box was opened. I received a nasty letter of "we're not interested and for other reasons". I reported the response to the four-member department and we all agreed to proceed. After back and forth negotiation, we discussed this issue in the curriculum committee and the Chicana chair of social science sent her older men, basically mocking my course on Central Americans

with comments such as, "they are such a small percentage in total U.S. population" and "how many Central Americans do we really have!" I responded emotionally and aggressively! The attack
was beyond intellectual discourse, it was insulting real student
need and my extensive effort. From that point on, I now had a permanent enemy. It didn't help that she (chair of social science) was
also the chief contract negotiator for the district and partially
funded many campaigns of the local trustees members with her
disc-jockey husband.

From this point on, my departmental members began to question my efforts though this was agreed upon collectively. As the
youngest instructor in the department and the campus, I started at
age twenty-six, I also developed a close repoire with students.
First I was approachable, second, I was caring and humanistic and
lastly, I was trying to enhance the department. In my first four
years, I had written six new courses and probably could have had
ten, had there not been opposition from social science and then
the earth science departments. Except for the course on Chicano
Gangs, the three other courses mentioned were shelved and have
not been revisited.

My courses became popular because I could relate from shared
experience, shared age and shared interests. There was an interest
because I knew my material, acknowledged when I didn't and in-
corporated their lives as equal knowledge to the books. This strat-
egy has been my success. Enrollment skyrocketed in my classes
and I never rejected anybody. I became some kind of role model
and part-time counselor with students my age for both genders.
The department took this as too friendly and having crossed
boundaries. I even pushed my responsibilities with a city tour I
learned from Mike Davis. We went through skid-row, Bunker hill,
McArthur Park, to Lennox and the underground school.We attended plays, Virgen de Guadalupe mass at 3:00 a.m., camping
and even went to a Chicano gay club, the Arena.

Each field trip brought the students together. Most of the excursions were originally suggested by students, plus it was a way
of learning outside of the classroom. Then the avalanche began as

I was being evaluated in my third year. The two previous evaluations were all satisfactory from both faculty and students. The third is when I began to be accused of improprieties and then I heard that I was "too arrogant". "You think you know it all", the literature expert would say, then I would hear, "perception is reality". I was guilty of sensuality. The chair, who I had helped promote, began to try to monitor my every move. First, I was dismissed as evening chair, though I spent most of the time on campus and then I was memorandum to death: For not returning a video another adjunct faculty had borrowed, a slide projector I was told to hold on to for the summer and even for using more than three books in my history classes. Then I was accused of teaching too many subjects, though when they had a shortage, I was asked to teach it. The onslaught was horrendous because I was still on probation and any retaliation would be construed as me being uncooperative. It was a no-win situation.

When the first evaluation came that December of 1998, in the meeting, I was chewed up and spat on. The literature expert kept accusing me of academic deficiency and as a receptor of false allegations I fought back. He was even trying to get me to debate themes in my evaluation. I knew then, he had gone overboard and I ignored his statements. He resigned as chair of my evaluation committee. Though I kept hearing "you think you're too arrogant", plus I had seen this rejection of other young instructors already, thus I was cautious. This same literature expert on a few occasions in front of me, basically told off a young adjunct Chicano faculty member who was completing his Ph.D. in education at UCLA. When this same person applied for a full time position, the other instructor, the "always leaving character" stated in a sixties vato slang accent, "we ain't gonna hire that motha fucken arrogant son of a bitch". Without doubt he was the best candidate, but the old timers excluded him and any suggestion he had even for adjunct faculty. The literature "expert" also told a Peruvian young woman who was interested in teaching; she had to be a Chicana to teach in Chicano Studies. He had now crossed into intra-ethnic and gender discrimination. I tried to mitigate his comment by instantly telling her to apply and that I would try to get her approved. This other doctoral student never did follow up. The young adjunct Chicano instructor later asked me what was the problem with the old timer and that he had previously behaved in a similar fashion. I understood but couldn't do much other than encourage them to apply. The old timers held the real hiring power. Not to personally attack, though this individual is continuously accused of being senile with the administration doing nothing to remedy or seek help on his behalf. Another young Chicano male was also excluded from permanent hire in the math department by an older Chicano, (former chair of the math department) because he was a "know it all". Luckily, he was hired in a tenure track position at Santa Monica City College with higher pay, though his heart was set at teaching at his alma mater. He was accused of being a young buck and he paid dearly. In a department of ten plus full time instructors, there is only one Chicano (the old timer mentioned) with 95% of the students being Chicanos. Such action was not fair and he left!

When my evaluation ended, I was placed on probation and assigned a mentor. My mentor met with me every week and we talked, discussed, outlined goals, ideals and so forth. She told me I was not the problem. I knew I wasn't but I was accused of being arrogant. I went through a second evaluation and because I did not admit to being 50% wrong, I was placed on continued evaluation for another semester. In my four years at ELAC, I have not known any instructor to go through such green-beret evaluation. My student evaluations had been consistent, a 95% approval rating and I was still accused of being academically deficient.

I went through their process and won. I was recommended for tenure and six weeks later, the administration strong-armed two faculty members to change their vote to recommend my tenure. I have been exhausting my legal remedies, but in the process of grievance, the vice president of academic affairs accused me of being "arrogant and if I won, that I would snub them in the air". The union representative told him such claim was not in the contract and had no validity. Nonetheless they have proceeded with termination!

This whole experience has taught me and through observation, that young faculty are held to double standards unlike themselves. I was accused of tardiness, though my office is next door to my classroom and the president acknowledged in front of the union official that all faculty members were tardy to their classes. Thus, I am being held to the utmost of double standards with no regard to my due process. Along the way as I have sought legal remedy, I learned that there are no laws that protect young people. Though I could get four or five young adjunct faculty to testify, legally I can not hold the college responsible for such repugnant action. Worse yet, men have no other recourse. Women have flexibility with sexual harassment though we have no protection, and not even in sexual harassment, somebody has to make advances for it to be sexual harassment. Ethnic discrimination is just as hard to prove.

When I approached older Chicano faculty I was denied assistance even from such foundation. My support has come from non-Chicanos, especially from Black and Asian Studies. As we organized to address the board of trustees, in three consecutive meetings, there were fifteen young and older students, both males and females there to testify on my behalf and for those future students who will be the most effected.

The older students were the first to admit in their testimony that I was facing age discrimination and that such action should not be tolerated because Chicano students were being left out of the benefit to collectively learn.

When I mentioned this issue to my colleague in the math department at Santa Monica College, he instantly stated he wanted to discuss how he was told "you young bucks have an attitude problem". The beneficiaries of the sixties Chicano civil rights movement are the ones who are discriminating younger people for the sin of being born in 1969. Little do they know, I also protested the Gulf War, Panama, Proposition 187 and other challenges of the 1990's. As Adriana Aguirre, a sixth grade English and Social Science studies teacher at South Gate Middle School, also known as the most crowded in America, states, "It's a cultural class expectation of one having to pay their dues, though the George Bushes of America don't. Though, working class Chicanos have to." She also indicates how as a young teacher at both elementary and middle schools, the young instructors are being blamed for the failure of education, though it's the older faculty who are there to only pick up a paycheck". Young teachers are given the students most in need, work in the most impoverished communities and are the ones who are bilingual and most willing to participate in extra curricular activities. She wants to start an association entitled the "New Teacher's Alliance" because there is no infrastructure in existence to protect young teachers from harassment and from media negativism about the profession of education. She believes in all honesty, the older teachers gave up years ago and should retire, there is more damage being committed to Chicano students with a person who does not want to be teaching brown or black kids. This argument is also visible in collective bargaining agreements that should protect all paying dues members, though those with more "seniority" normally get compensated more than young people. Remember, all have to pay union dues.

Unions exist to protect the member with job security, increase in wages and protection from an unjust management system. Second, all management has dictatorial rights over the employee, because of weak labor laws. In my first year at ELAC, there was a union contract negotiated with the district. There was a pay increase, though it benefited those members with more seniority. The semester increase was not really an increase. The funds originated from a 20% cut in summer teaching income. Those who always taught in the summer were the young faculty who never earned enough to sustain them through the year. The campus union representative stated to me, "faculty get paid too much and now they cry for lost money, please!" The loser here was me! I was working the same and really more afterward to maintain what I had, while many retired with a golden package and their retirement is based on the last three highest income years. This union contract benefited them at young instructor's expense. We are then made to feel blessed because we are teaching at a coveted institution.

This experience of being singled out is not in a vacuum and many others feel the same. At every level, young folks have to over prove themselves and it never will be enough; is this a vital rite of passage? If it is, I want nothing to do with it.

P.S. In January of 2002, the faculty guild (AFT 1521) refused to legally represent me in the arbitration case. I lost the case even though eight students, two faculty members and the ex-grievance director testified on my behalf. Due process was useless!

Chapter Seven

The Betrayal

In my opinion, Chicanos, especially immigrant and ascending middle class Mexicans have betrayed our future. You might say I'm crazy, but hear me out. When many immigrant Mexicans arrived in Los Angeles, the one institution that never rejected them at the door was public education reaffirmed through years of civil rights struggles by previous Chicano-Mexicano families. Instantly children, including me, were taken in and a valuable education was attempted. The odds were great and almost impossible, mono-lingual Spanish-speaking children with many parents having had a less than 6th grade education from Mexico was the educational background most of our parents brought to the table.

Do not misunderstand me, I'm not saying we did not belong, because our parents paid for the education and had paid for, generations back and futuristic, our single most important investment. My great-grandfather had migrated from Guanajuato at the turn of the century and labored in the fields in Texas, Colorado and eventually in Los Angeles. He would migrate back and forth, until his final years of life. Hell, I make no apologies my grandfather had cousins born in Pueblo, Colorado who fought in World War I and nephews in World War II. We have been Americans all our lives. What I am stating is from observations of my generation who went to the Belmonts', Los Angeles, adult education, Lennox and the Garfield High Schools, is once Chicanos have achieved great success (this varies according to the individual), the offspring are then sent to private Catholic or Christian schools.

My definition of great success is the acquisition of educational tools that enables one to acquire white-collar decent salary employment. Most Chicanos do not complete their Bachelor of Art degrees but have had enough college preparation to be successful and many are. One particular example, my ex-brother and sister-in- law are employed in a law firm, where he specialized in computer network and she was a software specialist. These tools were acquired through K-12 education and they opted not to attend college. Nonetheless, they had enough preparation to be successful, purchase a home, etc. They have two children with an age difference of seven-eight years. Their combined income with only one child was probably three times more than her father's income in a year, yet he supported a family of eight. In my case, I annually make four times more than my mother and father ever did. My generation has become the success story our immigrant parents aspired us to be. Many did not obtain a college degree, yet they are still successful.

When many went to high school, there were problems and will always be, rather the school attempted the best for Chicanos. Obviously there were inadequacies as is dictated by limited public funding imposed by White California voters in 1978. In addition, there exist racial class differences that attributed to many under funded schools, the models of failure based on people's property values to fund education. The value of Mexicans is inferior to that of our white suburbs. Simultaneously, this does not mean we abolish these institutions rather we attempt to remedy them. But when it comes to education, "extra cash Chicanos", do negate those challenges. My mother, though limited in English and with only a 5th grade always participated in our education, volunteered for field trips, assisted in head start pre-schools and attended every sporting event my brothers and I were part of. My mother defends our high school, Hawthorne, to the tee, because she feels schools are not the problem. The real problem lies in the parents' lack of involvement or unappreciation of the school and the easy exit to a private institution of learning. Nonetheless, when per pupil funding in California ranks at number 41 nationwide and there is an attempt at quantifying racism through the Stanford 9 as Professor Ron Schneck of Woodbury University and Dorsey High School professes, there is a problem. The question arises, have we given up on public education?

Case in point, a good friend of my mother sent her son to Bishop Montgomery High School in Torrance because it was a "better" school, yet the kid was expelled because of a failing grade point average. My mother tired of hearing Leticia complain about how inadequate Hawthorne High was, yet she never bothered to learn about their academics. My problem with public education is their lack of ethnic studies within the curriculum, over-concentration on math and science and refusal to accept instruction in multi-languages. English, only! They deny the social sciences, humanities and the arts. My talent in social science was not stimulated, appreciated nor applauded yet I am now a college professor as a result of my interest in the social science.

A third example is a 26-year-old single father who sends his daughter to a parochial school. He believes this avenue will be her only opportunity for success. He believes Garfield High School in East Los Angeles failed him, but he doesn't acknowledge his parents' lack of formal education had much to do with his inability to learn the essentials. My mother's lack of English and math probably delayed my advancement in reading or writing, though I was able to learn. My mother, nonetheless, inspired and encouraged me to learn. She instilled a culture of education and my regular outings were to the Inglewood Public Library on Saturdays and after school.

Lastly, a member of my department sent his daughter to an all-girls Catholic school and when she opted for community college, she chose Mt. San Antonio College in the ritzy suburbs of the San Gabriel Valley over East Los Angeles or Rio Hondo College which are considered to be inferior because of the community they serve. Our own faculty in Chicano Studies perpetuates this class difference. This particular faculty member also sent his son to a Catholic High School in Orange County, a 20-mile one-way drive.

Our failure and neglect as mature adults has been to not hold school districts accountable to our children. Many parents remove their kids and place them within a certain class structure, demonstrated through private schools where all kids originate from similar economic backgrounds. We gringos -gringos come in brown, black, yellow and pale colors-institutionalize educational plight. Chicanos are creating the identical class divisions of poor versus rich schools. Color is relative. These children are too good to be with the masses, but when they were the masses, they complained about inequality.

I firmly believe because Chicanos make up the majority of the new demographic growth in the state of California. Nine out of ten Latinos in Los Angeles County are Chicanos (we are after all in Northern Mexico). We are planting the seeds of destruction in the public education system. The voucher system will probably be re-introduced because "extra-cash" Chicanos believe their children to be better than recent immigrants from Mexico. We are creating elitism among our own and turning our back on the one institution that can provide equality for many poor families. There is no difference in the model of white flight versus Chicano flight. The American dream!

Malinchistas, traitors instead of demanding equity! If we demanded equity in our schools, even white families would send their children to the eastside (A former student of mine who was enrolled in Jaime Escalante's math courses would hear from white kids how they wish they could attend Garfield High School in East Los Angeles). I truly believe this was why busing failed; schools in poor communities were never improved.

This is the ultimate betrayal towards our future, including my children and grandchildren. This American dream must be re-evaluated and altered, otherwise, when California becomes primarily Chicano and experiences decades of semi-governance, there will be future generations revolting not against the white establishment but the Chicano elite and this society will be torn down by class warfare. This plight already exists, through the militarization of the local police force. Many new officers who are Chicanos are instantly willing to put a bullet in this teenage kid they have identified as "unreformable". This is seen through the Rampart police scandal where many Latino officers have been involved in illegal framing of such individuals. The local Chicano politicians have done nothing to question this violation of civil rights. According to the *Los Angeles Times* article on such nonresponse, even County Supervisor Gloria Molina commented, "These were not the best of citizens", though the paralyzed individual, Honduran by birth, did not have a criminal record. Where does the assumption of innocence exist after the very judicial establishment that framed him, removed his ability to walk, and caged him up for three years? What I am trying to point out, the class position asserted through some minimal gain will occur at the expense of poor Chicano/Latinos. The Rampart scandal proves my point. Senator Tom Hayden from the Westside created more noise than any of the local Chicano elected officials.

This class difference is what will force many to ask themselves, does it matter if there is a Chicano/Latino elected official? The answer based on past evidence could mean probably no, though I do not want to generalize because these issues are more complex and people (Chicano politicians) might be strong on other issues.

Until people as a whole, especially "extra-cash" Chicanos, demand equity in education, there will exist a class division that will continue to tear down public education as we know it. Polarization will then be the norm and the Compton K-12 district might become the statewide model in conjunction with state prisons in Calipatria and Ocotillo.

Chapter Eight

The Honest Truth about Sexual Prowlness: Chicanos & Chicanas Are Alike

As a young man, I was led to believe that men were more sexual than women. We men had an innate characteristic that the penis was always on the lookout and it always is. Moreover, we were at least socialized to be a hunter. As soon as we smelled the prey, it was then our time to move in. Success was never a guarantee but the intent to do, act "male" was; the hunter was considered more valiant than being rejected.We young boys would eventually learn from trial and error on how to approach a woman. It was never easy. The fear of rejection was so great, at times trying was not worth it. One even internalizes self-esteem either positively or negatively based on the feedback from a woman. I failed in that aspect early on.

Now women were socialized to protect their "value"; "*su respeto*", was determined on how often they let themselves go or perceived to be let go. Women had the one thing *coyotes* wanted. However, I learned that women were also coyotes. This ideal of vulnerability was relative. Women had to learn to be defensive because of the *zopilotes*, vultures.Women were overprotected because the zopilotes would not stop flying around. Once she let go, it was generally over. She lost *su respeto*.

Ironically, one was expected to be *un "hombre"* through *mujeres* though, women were being taught to stay away because they ultimately had the last say. Thus, for the males, we entered the

stage of endless natural desires of coveting a woman. Woman, indirectly though, had the same desire: To covet the *calor*, warmth
of a male; what the opposite sex offered. This was to be learned
only through experience, though each gender group had different
standards. Men hypocritically were given the green light, both
older males and females, it was condoned by mothers, fathers, if
they were around, and females. Mothers and fathers because their
boys were becoming men. For females the experience provided a
secured notion of the future.

Women were also given the green light reluctantly, though as if
it was turning yellow. Mothers were hesitant because they knew
that if pregnancy came, the child would remain with the mother,
a premature responsibility. Even if mothers advocated for an
abortion, they comprehended that this *"pesadilla"*, nightmare
would be shouldered by the daughter. Because these burdens
would solely fall on the daughters, the mothers were applying
double standards that seemed unfair, but realistic from their lived
experiences. Most men ran out versus the women leaving.

This outlook of life resulted in females being socialized to de-
sexualize themselves as much as possible. The values imposed
were to not be sexually aggressive or open. The value system
ranged from the chastisement of a *"piruja"* to not desiring sex that
much. Women were made to believe that they could go without
sex for months or even years. Many abide by these values.
Though ironically when the pregnancy comes, which generally
does so before the wedding, the strict social control ceases to ex-
ist.Young women then might become more cautious of the sexu-
ality and emotional connection that exists.Thus families protect
their females through their value system. Men on the other hand
are not as protected.Men are taught to be vulnerable and gypsy-
like. They can exist with no attachment to either a child or the person whom he procreated with. Men are truly the vulnerable ones.
They have no physical connection as the female does to their fe-
tus and it is of no coincidence that the father can detach himself
quite easily.Though there are enough women who do abandon
their newborns in record numbers to make one question if even

women and motherly roles are also not just gender impositions. The mothers are the only ones who truly protect their men because *"ellas los parieron"*. They gave birth to the males. Thus women are indirectly protected from sex until it is naturally impossible. Except for some young girls with children, most succeed. When age and responsibility cease to matter, females become just as sexually open, though still façade themselves under this veil value system. Most young men seek out older women because they are most open, mature and play less mental games. Many young men are sexually introduced to life by older women, generally ten to twenty years older. I'm of the belief that "sexual education" should be taught by older women and not older men. Why? The older women know their bodies and motions better. When a woman comprehends that she gives herself an orgasm, the male is introduced into a world most men don't comprehend.

Sadly, because sex and body was de-emphasized, younger women normally comprehend their orgasms only through experiences. When a woman expects the man to give her an orgasm, the ignorance of both on their parts can be emotionally catastrophic. Older women seek out younger males because there is a wealth of knowledge she can use as a skill to seduce herself. This is a seduction through "tenderness, caressing and experience". Experience becomes a power! Many equate this to motherly sex, but this is not an incestual relationship, rather of security young women can not match. Older women know this and they exploit the clay that is now going to be spinned for configuration. Oddly, if the social values that held younger women existed, why do older women act more "male"? It has to do with age. These women are older, have probably had their own children and now have nothing to lose. They have gained through life.They have much to offer and young men have endless energy, as I have heard many say. Better yet, older women have learned that they don't need to hang on to a man to have sex. They know these young adults will probably not hang around if they are twenty years younger. Sooner or later, the male will want children and a comparable person. Sexually, this is liberating for older women. Not that a young man is

a passerby, though realistically they are. Older women comprehend that they will not cling on to a specific partner, thus living
through this experience is not as traumatic. Eventually the memories become a memory bank both genders will carry with life.
Though the focus has been on the older female, but the young
male cherishes this for life, too.

With the older female, the male learns to make love or have sex
mentally free. Performance is relative as long as one is open to
suggestions. This is the one opportunity the male can give in and
be free.An open acceptance, an endless learning process. (The
young male cherishes his lust of his sixth grade teacher come
alive or beauty in semi-aged skin, where youth is secondary).

Both experience what they want for that moment. The fifty-
year-old grandmother who re-defines the definition of *abuela*; the
woman whose daughters are old enough to be dated by the male;
the gray-haired woman who is not effected by gravity; the gray
hair which is just as sexual versus the non-aged hair; the forty-
five-year old who lies about the new sexual positions and the pos-
sessive woman who becomes livid because the male moves on.
These sexual relationships do not ignore emotions. They develop
because of emotions, though the gender animals run according to
their fears. The fear of having to give more and the fear of want-
ing more. Most sex is emotional. It stops being emotional when
either person wants no more from that specific person, whether
young or old.

Most believe the male is unfaithful and maybe nine out of ten
are, yet the female is just as unfaithful or slightly less. The female
is unfaithful eight out of ten times. Not much difference from the
male. The male is blunt, incapable of lying. They were never
forced to live in secrecy unless they were homosexuals. Women
were always forced to live with secrecy. The good girl versus the
bad girl! The male was expected to be whoring, *se tiene que ser
hombre.* Even women were uncomfortable about an inexperi-
enced man. They at least wanted to be talked to by an experienced
man. Women developed skills in double lives. An "innocent"
looking woman was not expected to be sexual though she was

more than lived. Women learned to lie and lie good. They could sense the man when he was venturing off. The most minimal detail is observed. Is there a difference in a speech pattern, habits, even in sex? Internally the woman knew, but the man didn't.

The man has been conditioned to believe the female a saint, pure, innocent, incapable, of evil deeds. The woman would never lie, so we were misled. Just as the male believes himself not able to be monogamous, the female knows she is also not. She attempts as does the man, but the temptations of life are too much. For women, attacks are constant. The so-called "more prettier" even more offers, but they are used to this. They are desired not because they can offer mental or spiritual soothing, rather a warm spot of release. The shallowness of men and women comprehend this, until someone captivates them. A particular smile, attraction, laugh or just a break from the daily routine will suffice for succumbing to temptation. Women have this power! The power of the vagina! In Mexico I learned a saying, *"un dicho: que puede mas, brazos or piernas"*. What has more power, legs or arms? The legs and women know this.Men approach them and women can control the si or no, if this is not violently violated.

The power to pick or choose becomes normal but females never cease to forget this attribute. For men, to go somewhere else where the power is being shared is the only power they have. And still they must be given permission. Any yes is normally accepted because rejections are more frequent. Men have endless reasons to be unfaithful, though the same applies to women. Thus as both humans crave other humans, they also act just the same in saturating those urges. Women both married and unmarried cheat quite similar to males, but they hide it better.

One sees the woman who lives with her husband but can have sex with another friend; the female who states she is with her best male friend while they engage in an alley or park; a second marriage woman, who brings her sex partner over and uses the condoms in her husband's drawer, an attempting to reconcile *mujer* who spends the night with her male friend while she thinks life over; an always breaking up girlfriend who cannot leave her partner but has unprotected sex; a woman who openly accepts that her lover has a long-term girlfriend and makes the excuse that he is not married to her; a girlfriend who uses vengeance to get back at her partner; an unsure girlfriend tempted to do it but holds back more because of upbringing guilt versus it's not right to do this to him; a roommate who has felt lonely and settles for the closest and least threatening penis though knows he's involved and so forth.

Men and women are thus both alike. These scenarios easily account for both genders. Both are responsible. Though it questions one to comprehend if this is truly how life is. To have multiple partners and not be monogamous. Ironically biologically we are different, with different organs but with complementary tasks yet, genetically, during the first five weeks, all men are females until the genes develop. Could the answer exist there in our commonalties versus our differences? How could it not? This is what shapes us for the rest of our existente. We need to be more honest and accepting of our similarities versus differences because we act too similar to ignore this fact.

Lastly, the most liberating partner is one that is psychologically free of external and internal judgment. We complement each other greatly sexually, whether young or older.

Chapter Nine

An Alternative Home: Non-Mexicans Finding Acceptance Among Mexicans

NATIONAL GEOGRAPHIC MAGAZINE

People from North and Central America have the same genetic structure not found anywhere else in the world. Though many ethnicities, cultures and languages exist, these people are genetically from the same father. (This article uses Bering Straights theory as origin)

SPIRIT OF THE JAGUAR (PBS DOCUMENTARY)

Many of the lives that now exist in Central America or what is known as MesoAmerica, migrated from South America or from North America. Whether the sloth, Quetzal, turtle or deer.

Many western anthropologists keep insisting on the Bering Straights Theory (that our ancestors migrated from Mongolia across the Ice Bridge dividing Alaska from Russia and migrated south throughout the Western Hemisphere), though endless discoveries of evidence pinpoint in another direction. Whether in Chile, Brazil, Mexico, the American Southwest or Central

America, the remains prove that people were already here. Jack Forbes in *Aztecas del Norte*, page 17–18 further states;

"Nevertheless, most general historical works dealing with the United States are concerned almost solely with a single perspective, that of the Anglo-American or English-speaking European. As important as this latter viewpoint is, it cannot explain the development of the Native American cultures, the Hispano-Mexican influence, or the presence of some 8,000,000 Mexican-Americans in the United States. In brief, it cannot explain the history of the Southwest; and because it cannot explain all of the various parts, it cannot elucidate the whole (Fawcett Publications, 1973).

Though the publication is twenty-six years old and the numbers of Chicanos in the United States has exploded to 30 million, we are nonetheless viewed as foreigners, both in historical and contemporary times. Yet, as the east (U.S. East Coast and Europe is east from California; writers) attempt to de-legitimize our Native American existence, we need to view our space in relation to other groups of people.

In the present, Chicanos are now being labeled "Latinos" or "Hispanics", which implies some connection to the Latin world of Rome. Personally I have never been to Rome thus I do not see the connection or affiliation. Everybody in my family was born in the American Southwest or in Central Mexico (maternal grandparents). Therefore if much is not known about our Native American existence, then why are we lumped in with the worlds of Italians, Spaniards or Portuguese?

The argument has centered on our usage of "Spanish" therefore are we Latin Americans? Should the U.S. then be considered a Latin country because the speaking population here is greater than those countries of Colombia or Argentina, considered some of the largest in Latin America? And in fifty years with the continued demographic growth, there will be more Spanish speaking people here than in Spain. Will that make us Spaniards? No, we will become more Mexican or Native American than we actually are willing to admit that we are (think about the food, who is raising who and the origin of the Southwest, plus who is having more children).

Therefore, I do not believe we should be labeled "Latinos" or "Hispanics" because we use a dialect of Latin. We also use English as a common day language, does that make me English? Are the Irish or Scottish English because they speak in English? Of course not. Then we see what Jack Forbes states, that Mexicans in the United States are not understood and it starts with the identification of them. Census-wise Mexicans are considered white, because we were legitimized as cheap labor. Therefore, if we are not Latinos our identification must be tied into the historical struggle of a people and culture.

Chicanos therefore, must be called Chicanos or Mexicans independent of the rest of Spanish speaking people. Why? Because our history is tied to this land, this space, this place and not continents away. Simultaneously, other Spanish-speaking people need to be identified with their struggles. Boricuas, people of Puerto Rico or Nuyoricans must be given their historical place because by being lumped in with everybody else, their status as a living colony is de-emphasized. Their struggle to rid the US Navy from Vieques is rendered useless and obsolete. The same occurs with people from El Salvador, Honduras or Guatemala. When everybody is lumped as one, "these people are then viewed as foreigners". Case in point, for over four decades, Cubans have been treated preferentially over Mexicans. My mother was born twelve miles from the Calexico border. Or better said, she was born on the US but not inside. Because of this status, she was forced to be a "mojada", though her grandfather had worked in Los Angeles at the turn of the century and had cousins born in Colorado, Kansas and in other regions of California. My mother was treated as a preferential criminal and when not needed at times expelled or not permitted to visit her own daughter for over three years.

Cubans on the other hand were given residential cards, housing, welfare and other comparative advantages many Mexicans did not receive. Even me as a citixen was treated worse than any Cuban who has arrived in the U.S. When I was younger I saw how we (Chicanos) were always much poorer than Cubans, though we were all US born. We worked just as hard and never got anywhere. We lived in this reservation called Lennox though many Cubans, especially the white Cubans, would own homes and receive food stamps simultaneously. My mother could not receive food stamps because of social security so she went to the damaged packaged food store. Thus, one views that history is tied directly to a people.

As Chicanos and other Native American people have struggled to survive the onslaught of European America, we have done so through, violence, racism, poverty and as endless second class urban or rural peasants, even if somewhat educated.

To be continuously ignored has resulted in an endless Brown World, no different than being in central Mexico. Because we have been misidentified, mis-categorized, missed period. We then find ourselves becoming two lives. One present and one past! The present life has been to become "Anglo". Therefore as we have become "Brown Gringos" (term quoted from *Drink Cultura*) we act Anglo. We have become bigoted and prejudicial. How many Mexican parents do not want their daughters to date a "mayate"? The consolidation is that they don't want their daughters dating somebody from Oaxaca, too short. How many apple pie Cholos are not afraid to admit hating Blacks or Chinos? The comforting aspect is that not many Chinese or Blacks want their kids dating Mexicans either. This is Equal Opportunity America for one. Thus Blacks and Asians are also Anglos. We're all Anglos, but racism excludes. Not that I want to be Europeanized either. This admission is what makes one an American. Simultaneously, it is fair to state, that the past is still alive in us.

When the Christians, whether the Spanish or English arrived, they were fairly welcomed. The Aztecs practically opened the door to Cortez, the Chumash in California greeted Serra quite benevolently until it was too late and the Pilgrims were saved from their ignorance by the local people and see how they were repaid. This open acceptance still resonates and is visible through other racial ethnicities in Los Angeles, though the openness of people has been curtailed because of the psychotic-ness of distrust that exists in Los Angeles. Los Angeles is a very unfriendly place.

It is built on illegitimacy and slavery with a permanent under-class. That is me and others. Some might object to this general-ization though when 50% of the population is impoverished, that does include me and others who claim to be middle-class. Just be-cause we attend college does not mean we are not a paycheck away from homelessness. And though we pay a mortgage, if this is not paid timely, then we'll really see who owns what. And when your mother cannot afford to pay rent and counts her fifteen-dollar singles from tips of haircutting, you see that the impover-ished live among you. What happens if I die before my mother? Who will care for her?

This is the reality of Los Angeles, we are Native Americans and yet we have to buy our land back. If that isn't modern slavery, I do not know what it is. If you are lucky, you can purchase, other-wise you will remain a permanent slave unto a lord, a rent collec-tor whom they call a "landlord".

In Los Angeles we don't walk, much less talk to each other. Everybody fears somebody is out to pimp a dollar off of you and they are. We can't talk to people on the street for all kinds of rea-sons. Some legit, others not, it's just not part of the culture. Whereas from my travels in Mexico, people do talk, they greet each other, they say "hola", "buenos dias", "buenas tardes", "como esta", "como le va" and if you ask for a glass of water, it will generally be handed to you. Crime does exist, but that is an indicator of the economic environment. Even in the largest city of the world, I made friends on a bus and we still communicate from ten years back. My aunt once took my cousin's friend in in Mexicali when the young man had no place to stay and had re-cently been deported from the San Joaquin Valley. He stayed six months until his father picked him up from Guadalajara. She still wonders where's he at today. In el D.F. I asked a girl, how to take the metro and she wanted to have coffee. In L.A. if I greet a woman, she looks at me strange. People clamor for a place to so-cialize in Los Angeles at. Schools or the work place is where one has the best opportunity. There is no such thing as a plaza, so-cially speaking in L.A. Cholos (American apple pie) socialize better than anybody; they are not afraid of the street, then again, they have few choices.

But that hope of comprehending yourself results in a search of acceptance. And because Mexicans/Chicanos make up the foundation but are on the outside, we also become a place of refuge for anybody who wants to enter. Here we want to talk, if anybody is willing to open up to us. And because all ethnic groups are provincial, anybody outside the provinciality, even among themselves can result in an exclusion. Therefore it is easier to relate to somebody who has experienced a similar exclusion.

In California, Chicanos have always lived in seclusion, not of our choice. The world outside believes California is blue-eyed when in reality it's brown-eyed. Therefore, one who migrates to California is shocked to learn that they might be migrating to Mexico, unless you move to beach communities. A Colombian woman once stated, "I did not know I was going to become Mexican in the U.S." Another Colombian/Chicano teacher at South Gate Middle School mentions that his sister was a chola in Huntington Park with her raccoon-eyed makeup and dickies pants. Another Colombian/Chicano male student stated, "My sisters were some of the biggest home-girls in Echo Park." If you were to tell them they were not Mexicans, they would refute that. This is their adopted identity and who is to argue with them?

A Salvadorian kid raised in Boyle Heights states he is Chicano because he grew up in the barrio. A Vietnamese-Korean woman who attended Inglewood High School finds acceptance with her Mexican best friend's family because her own relatives saw her as an outsider. My brother's best friend, an Okinawan from birth by his mother and his Alabaman white father feels more at home with my mother than either native group. A Bolivian woman whose daughter was born in Los Angeles asks", Is my daughter a Chicana?" And how can one reject such a claim. A Black Cuban who uses the word "chingar" but can't pronounce the "R" and lives in Lennox, a Mexican reservation or a Bolivian born Chicana (she enrolled in Chicano Studies courses) states to her father that Mexican history needs to be taught in schools because Chicanos are natives. He ponders isn't that like Chileans moving to Bolivia and demanding Chilean Studies. He states, "Forget it". No papi, this was once Mexico, the relation is different. It's like Bolivians demanding Bolivian Studies in Chile for having lost our coastal state.

A Chicanized white woman who talks better "Calo", *ora ese*, then states, I might not be a Chicana but I am carrying one inside me.A 1960 ex-revolutionary Communist member talking to a former colleague in "Calo" at UCLA prior to a Culture Clash show. They are both "white" in skin but not in culture. Simon eses! A Black Cholo, a Mexican, a Blexican who approaches my mother from my elementary years in Inglewood and talks to her in Spanish and gives her a big hug as if he was hugging his mother. A Peruvian who marries a Chicana and learns the Chicano definition of a cholo, unlike from Peru but not really. They are both seen as the unwanted.

Puerto Ricans via the father but never been to Puerto Rico much less New York, only Durango. A Salvadorian-born Chicano who was head of MECHA at UCLA in the early 1980's while leading protests against fraternities for mocking Mexicans and a Granada, Nicaragua- born family who reside in Boyle Heights gave me the definition of Nicaragua, "hasta aqui llegamos". A Nahuatl term the Mexicas gave for this distant route trade. Culturally, they are both Nica-Mex as Angela Fajardo so eloquently states in her poem posted in her classroom at Lennox Middle School.Lastly, Guatemala, another Nahuatl term that means "place of many trees". *National Geographic* demonstrates we are originally one.

In Los Angeles because anybody who is Brown or has a Spanish surname is instantly assumed to be a Mexican also serves an alternative home. The quite frequent commonality is that non-Mexican people from Central American generally occupy the same living space, because socially they are economically similar.

One time I overheard Mike Davis say: "I once knew a female labor organizer in England who saw herself, as an Irish, female, Catholic, labor organizer, and so forth". He explained to us that people have multiple identities that they can chose from and it never has to be solely one."

If one thinks about nicknames associated with an individual's individuality, that makes perfect sense. The Aztecs would grant names based on one's progress in life.Therefore one never stopped being anything. They just augmented the different names to represent him or herself.

Likewise, just because I have mentioned people who have added an alternative home, this does not mean they have to give up their own natural identity. This would take away from their ability to adopt any other identity. One just builds upon what they have learned or shared with other people. The addition of other cultures is very much in line with Native American practice that I have studied or seen throughout my life. These are the shortcomings of homogenizing a people, their history and struggles, and not their true connection as united and ever-evolving cultures shaped by both internal and external factors. Therefore, people are one in foundation but ever growing simultaneously.

Thus, I see myself, as a Mexicano Purempecha-Mayo-Cachanilla-Mexican-Native American who cannot be simplified by having been originally from another continent or easily compartmentalized as a "Latino, Hispanic or American". These labels ignore who I truly am, plus one can always find a home with us.

P.S. Sometime later, I will augment another identity because it is ever evolving.

Afterthought

To be introvert and extrovert was the principle aim of this body of work. I hope one takes in the following principles and thinks about how to redefine not just concepts, but attitudes of life. We carry negative but also positive attributes and only in this search will we find such answers.

The principles of each chapter are as follows:

We are not mestizos, but full-blooded Native Americans!
La virgen de Guadalupe should be called Tonantzin; but if you are
    an atheist, live on!
Both males and females are machos, it is about power!
Mexicans should stop subsidizing the Mexican elite.Do not send
    money to Mexico except for senior citizens and sick loved
    ones!
Mexican families need not be sugarcoated!
Chicano Movement Activists need to stop thinking they had the
    only struggle in the world!
Mexican families need to stop thinking they are White ala educa-
    tion. Support Public Education!
Chicano people: we are both sexual animals and let's not be
    hypocritical!

Lets be all inclusive as we have always been: if you think in terms
    of color, you have been mentally enslaved!
Love not hate one another!

Lastly, the search is to also initiate collectively, some new paradigm that will be independent of the "American Dream", (that
will never be) and identifies us not as future entrepreneurs,
clients, workers, customers or consumers, but as humans fighting
for a just society.

Notes

Burciaga, Antonio. *Drink Cultura.* (Santa Barbara, California, Joshua Odell,1995).

Davis, Mike. Personal Discussion in Pasadena, California; 1998.

Forbes, Jack D. *Aztecas Del Norte: The Chicanos of Aztlan.* (Greenwich, Conn: Fawcett Publications, 1973), 17–18.

National Geographic Society, October 1997. *Ancient Americans.*

Public Broadcasting System. 1999. *Spirit of the Jaguar: The Geographical Formation of Central America.*

Riccardi, Nicholas,."Latino Leaders Relatively Quiet on Rampart Scandal", *Los Angeles Times* 29 February 2000, 1.

www.ingramcontent.com/pod-product-compliance
Lightning Source LLC
Chambersburg PA
CBHW050526280326
41932CB00014B/2477